Smithsonian
Wild Animal
EXPLORER

TABLE OF CONTENTS

Meerkat
p. 38

Pufferfish
p. 174

Hippopotamus
p. 84

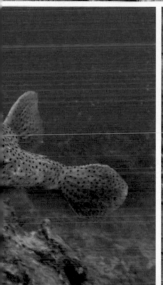

Jaguar
p. 220

Giant Panda
p. 266

Arctic Fox
p. 310

AMAZING ADAPTABLE ANIMALS

ANIMALS ARE ABSOLUTELY INCREDIBLE, HAVING ADAPTED TO LIVE IN EVERY ENVIRONMENT ON THE PLANET. YOU CAN FIND ANIMALS ON EACH CONTINENT, FROM THE DRIEST DESERT TO THE COLDEST TUNDRA, ON TOPS OF MOUNTAINS OR AT THE DARKEST DEPTHS OF THE OCEAN FLOOR.

WHAT IS AN ANIMAL?

Animals are organisms that have senses and can breathe, move, eat and reproduce. One of the biggest differences between plants and animals is that plants make their own food through photosynthesis, while animals must digest plants or other animals for food.

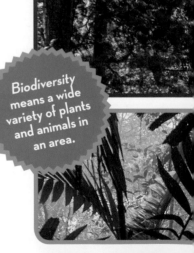

Biodiversity means a wide variety of plants and animals in an area.

DESERTS
are places with little
rainfall and vegetation.

GRASSLANDS
are areas that are mostly
covered in grasses.

WATER
includes oceans, lakes, rivers
and other bodies of water.

FORESTS
are largely covered with trees,
shrubs and other plants.

RAINFORESTS
are forests that get lots of rainfall
and have a lot of biodiversity.

POLES
are the North and South Poles.
Both are extremely cold and
covered in snow and ice.

UNDERSTANDING EVOLUTION

Why is it that some animals can withstand the incredible cold, while others can live underwater or fly in the air? Scientists say the answer is evolution!

The theory of evolution was first suggested by a scientist named Charles Darwin in 1859. Darwin said animals got their different traits through a process he called natural selection. According to natural selection, certain traits will be better for survival than others, and animals that survive have a better chance at reproducing and passing on those traits. Over a really long time—think thousands and thousands of years—the preferred traits will become standard traits for that species.

For example, animals that live in colder climates are more likely to survive if they

A scientific theory is not just a guess—it's a tested explanation that can be supported by a lot of evidence and facts.

can stay warm and hide from predators. That's why Arctic hares develop thick white coats in the winter—the extra fur keeps them warm and makes them harder to see in the snow. Any ancestors born without this ability probably didn't survive as well as those who were able to blend in. The concept of natural selection is sometimes referred to as "survival of the fittest."

DARWIN'S FINCHES

Darwin honed the idea of natural selection after visiting the Galapagos Islands and noticing the incredible variety in finches' beaks. On each island, the finches had different beak shapes—like large ones for cracking nuts or long ones for catching insects. This led Darwin to speculate the birds all had a common ancestor, but over time developed different beaks that were best suited to eating in their new environments.

DELVING INTO DESERTS

Deserts cover about 33 percent of Earth's land. They are places that get very little rain—10 inches or less per year!

Extraordinary Treasures

Deserts are always very dry, which leads to some extreme temperatures. They're usually very hot—in fact, the hottest temperature ever recorded was 134 degrees F in California's Death Valley. However, there are two big exceptions: the Poles! Both the Arctic and Antarctic regions are considered deserts.

WORLD

DESERTS ARE FOUND ON EVERY CONTINENT EXCEPT EUROPE. THE WORLD'S MAJOR HOT WEATHER DESERTS INCLUDE THE SAHARA IN NORTHERN AFRICA, THE KALAHARI DESERT IN SOUTHERN AFRICA, THE ARABIAN DESERT IN THE MIDDLE EAST AND THE GOBI DESERT IN ASIA.

WILD WORLD RECORDS

THESE DRY WEATHER CREATURES HAVE SOME AMAZING ADAPTATIONS.

MOST RESOURCEFUL
DUNG BEETLE
These insects use dung for just about everything.

MOST COMMON WILDCAT (IN THE U.S.)
BOBCAT
You might be shocked by this fact, but it's true! Because bobcats are nocturnal, you won't see them very often, but they're everywhere!

SMALLEST FOX
FENNEC FOX
They weigh less
than 3 pounds!

WEIRDEST SIPPER
THORNY DEVIL
Its special skin
collects water
from moist sand,
which travels to
their mouths!

BIGGEST LIZARD (IN THE U.S.)
GILA MONSTER
No wonder they call them
monsters!

FIVE FACTS ABOUT THE SAHARA DESERT

THE THIRD LARGEST DESERT AFTER ANTARCTICA AND THE ARCTIC, THE SAHARA COVERS AN INCREDIBLE 3.6 MILLION SQUARE MILES IN AFRICA.

1 The average summer temperature of the Sahara is above 100 degrees F.

2 You might think the desert all looks the same, but the Sahara has many different landforms: dunes, which are hills; ergs, which are also called sand seas; regs, which are made up of sand and gravel; hamadas, which are rocky plateaus; and salt flats, which are covered in sand, gravel and salt.

3 The Nile River made it possible for ancient people to live in the Sahara.

4 The Sahara used to have lots of plants but began to dry up 4,000 years ago as the tilt of the Earth's orbit changed. Scientists think it will be green again in about 15,000 years.

5 Sahara means "desert" in Arabic.

ARABIAN CAMEL

SCIENTIFIC NAME
Camelus dromedarius
LENGTH
Over 7 feet at hump
DIET Herbivore
LOCATION
Northern Africa,
Southwestern Asia,
Central Australia

Dromeus means "a runner" in Greek.

DESERT READY

No animal is equipped for the
desert quite like the camel:
Its nostrils can close to keep
out sand, and its extra bushy
eyebrows and long lashes serve
to protect its eyes.

Wild But True!

A camel's hump stores up to 80 pounds of fat, which it can break down into water and energy as needed.

Do you know how to tell if you're looking at an Arabian (dromedary) camel? Count the humps! Arabian camels have just one hump, while Bactrian camels, which are native to Central Asia, have two.

Dromedary camels were domesticated by humans about 3,500 years ago because they are incredible pack animals, able to carry big loads for up to 25 miles per day. They can also travel up to 100 miles without stopping for water!

ARMADILLO LIZARD

SCIENTIFIC NAME
Cordylus cataphractus
LENGTH 10 inches
DIET Omnivore
LOCATION South Africa

In Latin, *cataphractus* means "armored."

Covered in hard, bony scales, this lizard has great defense! When it feels threatened, the armadillo lizard rolls up into a ball and bites its tail, protecting its soft underbelly. By only exposing its scaly exterior, the armadillo lizard becomes pretty unappetizing to any predators looking for a snack.

Unlike many other lizards, armadillo lizards are fairly social and will rest together in groups of up to 30.

They take shelter in rock crevices, which is pretty clever! When they're wedged between two rocks and only presenting their backs, they're very well protected.

DUSKY DESIGN

This lizard's brownish-yellow scales help it blend into its desert environment.

Wild But True!

If a predator has caught an armadillo lizard by its tail, the lizard can shed it and grow a new one!

BLACK-TAILED JACKRABBIT

SCIENTIFIC NAME
Lepus californicus
LENGTH 2 feet
DIET Herbivore
LOCATION Central and
Western North America

Lepus is Latin for "hare."

Black-tailed jackrabbits are extremely fast. When being chased by a predator, jackrabbits will run in a zigzag pattern that is difficult to follow.

Despite living in the desert, these hares survive easily, thanks to their ability to eat just about any green they can find. They even eat rough desert plants like sagebrush or cacti. They also reproduce very quickly, giving birth to up to six leverets, or bunnies, a few times a year.

RAPID RABBIT

Jackrabbits can run up to 35 miles per hour and leap up to 20 feet at a time with the help of their strong legs.

Wild But True!

Technically, black-tailed jackrabbits are hares. Hares are born with fur and are bigger than rabbits, with taller back legs and longer ears.

BOBCAT

SCIENTIFIC NAME
Lynx rufus
LENGTH Up to 4 feet
(with tail)
DIET Carnivore
LOCATION
North America

In Latin, *rufus* means "red."

Bobcats weigh about 25 pounds, making them twice the size of most house cats. Though they're able to take down prey larger than themselves, they mostly hunt and eat smaller animals like rabbits, birds and rodents.

Bobcats are quite quick for their size, moving at speeds of up to 30 miles per hour. When on the hunt, bobcats advance by placing their back paws in the same spots where their front paws had been, making their movements as quiet as possible.

Wild But True!

Bobcats are often found in America's southwestern deserts, but they can also adapt to live in forests and swamps.

EXPERT EVADER

Even though the bobcat is the most common wildcat in the United States, people rarely see it because of its nocturnal habits.

23

CALIFORNIA KINGSNAKE

In Greek, lampros means "bright" and peltis means "shield."

SCIENTIFIC NAME
Lampropeltis getula californiae
LENGTH 2.5 to 6 feet
DIET Carnivore
LOCATION
Western United States and Northern Mexico

Though California kingsnakes have become popular pets, don't forget that they're wild animals! Kingsnakes are fierce hunters that got their name by besting other species of snakes—they often kill them for a meal.

California kingsnakes don't just eat other snakes, though. They also dine on small animals like lizards, mice and birds. These snakes are constrictors, meaning they squeeze prey to death and swallow it whole.

SPECIAL STRIPES

Most species of kingsnakes are banded, but California kingsnakes often have stripes that run along the length of their body.

Wild But True!

Kingsnakes are not venomous, but they are very resistant to venom from rattlesnakes, copperheads and cottonmouths.

DESERT

COYOTE

SCIENTIFIC NAME
Canis latrans
LENGTH
4 feet (with tail)
DIET Omnivore
LOCATION
North America

Latrans is Latin for "bark" or "roar."

While coyotes used to only live in North America's deserts and prairies, they've since adapted to life all over the continent. One of the reasons they thrive anywhere is because they'll eat just about anything, from rodents and rabbits to fish or snakes.

Coyotes are very social animals. They usually hunt in packs and choose a mate for life. Coyote pups are born in the spring, and both parents feed and protect their young until they are able to hunt on their own, usually by the following fall.

PERFECT PREDATOR

Thanks to their excellent senses of smell and sight (and the ability to run up to 40 miles per hour), coyotes are great at finding and catching their prey.

Wild But True!

Like their wolf cousins, coyotes communicate with a wide variety of yips, barks, howls and yelps.

DESERT TORTOISE

Gopherus comes from the French gaufre, meaning "waffle," and refers to the waffle or honeycomb-like chambers it builds underground.

SCIENTIFIC NAME *Gopherus agassizii*
LENGTH 9 to 15 inches
DIET Herbivore
LOCATION Southwest United States and Northern Mexico

The ground gets scorchingly hot where desert tortoises live—up to 140 degrees F. To stay cool, desert tortoises go underground. Using their forearms and nails, the reptiles dig burrows so they can escape the sun. Up to 25 desert tortoises may share the same tunnel, which can be more than 30 feet long.

The tortoises also use their digging skills to make grooves in the ground that will collect rainwater, enabling them to find a quick drink once they return to the surface.

TOUGH TORTOISE

When two male tortoises square off, they ram one another with the horns on their chests until one of the tortoises is flipped over, after which it will take him a lot of wriggling to right himself.

DUNG BEETLE

SCIENTIFIC NAME
Phanaeus vindex
LENGTH
0.2 to 2.4 inches
DIET Dung
LOCATION
Everywhere but
Antarctica

Vindex is Latin for "defender."

Dung beetles are incredibly resourceful with how they use dung—they eat it; they bury it underground and nest in it; and they even roll it into balls and use it to court their mates (a male will offer a ball to a female and if she accepts, they either roll it away together for nesting or he rolls it away while she rides on top).

This may all sound a bit gross, but you should be very thankful for dung beetles! They play a very important part in aerating soil and breaking down dung.

LIQUID DIET

Adult dung beetles eat by drinking the nutritious moisture in dung.

Wild But True!

Dung beetles are the first species known to navigate by using the Milky Way.

FENNEC FOX

SCIENTIFIC NAME
Vulpes zerda
LENGTH
9.5 to 16 inches
DIET Omnivore
LOCATION
North Africa

Zerda comes from the Greek *xeros*, meaning dry— a reference to the fox's desert home.

Weighing nearly 2.2 pounds, the fennec fox is the smallest species of fox. They're impressive jumpers for their size, able to jump 3 feet up from a standing position, and leap forward about 4 feet—a distance almost four times their length!

The nocturnal desert fox avoids the hottest part of the day by sleeping in an underground den, usually in a small group of up to 10 other foxes.

HELPFUL HAIR

While you'd think a lot of hair would be uncomfortable in the desert heat, the fennec fox finds it quite useful! Hairy feet protect its paws from scorching sand, while a thick coat insulates the fox during cold desert nights and protects it from the fierce sun during the day.

Wild But True!

The fennec fox's relatively giant ears radiate its body heat, helping it stay cool in the hot desert.

GILA MONSTER

In Latin, suspectum means "suspicious."

SCIENTIFIC NAME
Heloderma suspectum
LENGTH 21 inches
DIET Carnivore
LOCATION Southwest U.S. and Northwest Mexico

Gila (pronounced *hee-luh*) monsters are the biggest lizards native to the United States. They're also one of two lizards that are venomous. When a Gila chews on a victim, the venom moves through the grooves in their teeth to enter the open wound.

Despite this advantage, Gila monsters are very lazy hunters. They spend the majority of their time underground away from the desert sun, and only occasionally come up for food—usually stolen eggs or newborn mammals.

Wild But True!
A group of Gila monsters is called a lounge.

DESERT DIET

Gila monsters store a lot of fat in their tails, enabling them to go months between meals.

GILA WOODPECKER

SCIENTIFIC NAME
Melanerpes uropygialis
LENGTH 8 to 10 inches
WINGSPAN 16 inches
DIET Omnivore
LOCATION Southwest Coast of North America

In Greek, *melas* means "black" and *herpēs* means "creeper."

G ila woodpeckers use their long beaks to dig into cacti, where they can create cavities to live in. The shady, safe hole inside a cactus, called a boot, is the ideal place for them to raise their young.

These woodpeckers also have another interesting adaptation to cacti: their feet. Gila woodpeckers have two toes that point forward and two that point backward, enabling them to stand on vertical objects.

CREATIVE CALLS

Gila woodpeckers make many different noises, including yipping, a "*churr*" sound and a "*kee-u kee-u*" call.

Wild But True!
These birds are monogamous, preferring to have the same mate for as long as possible.

MEERKAT

Their Latin name means "to creep up or crawl up from below."

SCIENTIFIC NAME
Suricata suricatta
LENGTH 9.75 to 11.75 inches standing
DIET Omnivore
LOCATION
Southern Africa

A meerkat is a small species of mongoose famous for standing on its hind legs as it surveys the African plains. Meerkats live in large groups and work very well together. While a few stand guard, looking for signs of danger (and letting out a shrill call if they need to hide from a bird or other threat), the rest forage for their meals of berries, lizards and insects. Some meerkats will even act as babysitters for the newborns so their mothers can look for food.

BURROW BUILDER

Meerkats build extensive underground tunnel-and-room systems. By living underground, they're protected from larger animals and the hot sun.

Wild But True!

It's so cool in their tunnels that meerkats sleep in piles and begin each day with a sunbath to warm themselves up.

PRONGHORN

In Latin, *antilocapra* means "antelope-goat."

SCIENTIFIC NAME
Antilocapra americana
LENGTH 3.25 to 5 feet
DIET Herbivore
LOCATION
Western North America

Wild But True!

The pronghorn is the second-fastest creature on land, after the cheetah. Because of this, they can easily evade coyotes and bobcats.

Though its scientific name would make you think otherwise, the pronghorn is not a type of antelope—it's a whole different species! One of the biggest differences are the pronghorn's prongs, which are a cross between antlers and horns. They are the only creatures with forked horns that shed each year.

Both male and female pronghorns boast prongs, though the male's are much larger. You can also tell them apart by their fur markings: males have black markings that the females lack.

EXCELLENT EYES

A pronghorn can see a predator approaching from up to 4 miles away!

41

ROADRUNNER

SCIENTIFIC NAME
Geococcyx californianus
LENGTH 18 to 24 inches
WINGSPAN 19 inches
DIET Omnivore
LOCATION Southwestern U.S.

Coccyx comes from a Greek word which means "cuckoo."

Roadrunners can fly if they have to, but they generally prefer to stick to the ground, where they can run at speeds up to 20 miles per hour.

The roadrunner's most impressive feat is catching a rattlesnake for a meal: the bird snatches the snake by the tail and cracks it like a whip. Once the snake has died, the roadrunner swallows it whole, even though it takes a while to finish doing so—the bird just walks around with the rest of the snake hanging out of its mouth, continuing to swallow as it digests.

Wild But True!

To conserve energy, roadrunners will reduce their activity by 50 percent during the hot midday.

MOSTLY MEAT

Roadrunners prefer to be carnivorous, but will supplement their diet with plants during the winter when less prey is available.

SCORPION

SCIENTIFIC NAME *Scorpiones*

LENGTH 2.5 to 8.3 inches

DIET Carnivore

LOCATION Southern Asia, Europe and North America; Australia, Africa and South America

This name likely comes from the Greek *skerpo*, meaning "to pierce."

Scorpions are eight-legged arachnids, just like their cousins, spiders, mites and ticks. A scorpion mostly eats insects and uses its "telson," the venomous tip of its tail, to sting its prey.

When food is scarce, scorpions can reduce their metabolic rate so they require fewer meals. By doing this, some scorpions can eat as little as one insect per year!

Wild But True!
There are more than 2,000 different species of scorpions, but only 30 to 40 species have enough venom to kill a human.

SUPER SURVIVOR

Scorpions have been known to live through incredible conditions, including extreme temperature changes. In fact, researchers have frozen scorpions overnight and they lived—they simply thawed out in the sun and walked away the next morning.

TARANTULA

SCIENTIFIC NAME
Theraphosidae
LENGTH 4.75 inches
DIET Carnivore
LOCATION Tropical,
subtropical and
desert regions

This comes from the Greek word for wild beast, animal or monster.

Though 5 inches is already bigger than most spider-like creatures, a tarantula can seem even larger when it stretches out its hairy legs, giving it a span of up to 11 inches.

Unlike spiders, tarantulas do not use webs to catch their prey, and instead grab their meal (usually an insect) and bite it, injecting it with venom. The tarantula then secretes a digestive enzyme that will liquefy its meal, allowing it to be slurped up.

Wild But True!
A tarantula bite is certainly painful, but its venom is weaker than a bee's sting.

INCREDIBLE HEALER

When a tarantula molts (much like a snake does), it sheds its external skeleton. During this process, it can regrow internal organs and missing appendages.

THORNY DEVIL

SCIENTIFIC NAME *Moloch horridus*
LENGTH 6 to 8 inches
DIET Omnivore
LOCATION Australia

Horridus is Latin for "bristly" or "dreadful."

This spiky lizard has a neat trick: it uses its skin to collect and drink water! Dew forms on the spikes overnight, then moisture-attracting grooves between the lizard's "thorns" funnel the water directly to its mouth. More water can be collected by brushing against dewey grass and moist sand.

For food, thorny devils mostly eat ants—their sticky tongues are perfect for catching them. The thorny devil likes to sit near an ant trail and wait for a line of ants to cross in front of its waiting mouth!

Wild But True!

A thorny devil has a false head behind its real one! When threatened, it can tuck its real head down between its legs, presenting the fake head to a predator.

PUFFED UP

While the thorny devil's skin already serves as a deterrent to most predators, it can also inflate its chest to puff up its body, making it appear larger than it really is. That's why most predators think twice about trying to swallow one!

49

QUICK QUIZ
ARE YOU A DESERT EXPERT?

1 **What is a camel's hump filled with?**
   A. Water
   B. Fat
   C. Muscle

2 **Why do fennec foxes have such big ears?**
   A. To radiate body heat
   B. To swat flies
   C. To attract mates

3 **How do you pronounce "Gila," as in Gila lizard?**
   A. *Ghee-luh*
   B. *Hee-luh*
   C. *Jee-luh*

4 **Why do many desert animals burrow underground?**
   A. To escape the sun
   B. To avoid predators
   C. A and B

5 **How venomous is a tarantula?**
   A. It's one of the most venomous creatures on Earth.
   B. It's middle of the pack.
   C. Not very venomous at all.

6 **How do dung beetles navigate?**
   A. By looking at starlight
   B. By echolocation
   C. By scent

DESERT DELIGHTS

How can you tell which jackrabbits are getting old?
Look for the gray hares!

What steps do you take if a cougar is running toward you?
Big ones!

What do coyotes eat at the movies?
Pup-corn!

What do people do when they see a kingsnake?
They re-coil!

What do you call a crying camel?
A humpback wail!

What do you get when you cross a tortoise and a porcupine?
A slow-poke.

GETTING TO KNOW
GRASSLANDS

About one fourth of the planet's land is covered in grasslands!
They often occur between deserts and forests, and are
mostly flat with very fertile soil.

GRASSLANDS HAVE DIFFERENT NAMES AROUND THE WORLD AND ARE FOUND ON EVERY CONTINENT EXCEPT ANTARCTICA.

North America
PRAIRIES

South America
PAMPAS

Did you know?

While deserts have very little rainfall and forests have a lot, grasslands get just enough to grow many different kinds of grasses. Drier grasslands have grass that is 1 to 2 feet tall, while wetter ones may have grass as tall as 7 feet. But even the wettest grasslands do not get enough rain for a lot of tall trees to grow. To live in this area, a lot of animals are either grazers, like bison (p. 64) or zebras (p. 112), or animals that eat the grazers, like lions (p. 86).

TROPIC OF CANCER

EQUATOR

TROPIC OF CAPRICORN

WORLD

Europe
and Asia
STEPPES

Africa
**SAVANNAS
AND
VELDTS**

Australia
RANGELANDS

WILD WORLD RECORDS

GRASSLANDS HAVE SOME OF THE BIGGEST AND FASTEST ANIMALS IN THE WORLD—AND SOME OF THE SMELLIEST!

FASTEST LAND MAMMAL
CHEETAH

Reaching speeds up to 70 miles per hour, these cats could keep up with any car on the highway, if only for a moment.

LARGEST BIRD
OSTRICH

Standing up to 9 feet tall and weighing more than 350 pounds, these are some big birds! They also have the largest eyes of any animal on land.

SMELLIEST ANIMAL
SKUNK

With a musk that can even keep away bears, skunks are the smelliest of the grassland animals.

TALLEST ANIMAL
GIRAFFE

At 19 feet tall, giraffes tower over everyone else in the animal kingdom.

LARGEST LAND ANIMAL
AFRICAN ELEPHANT

Most of them weigh about 7 tons and some stretch 35 feet from trunk to tail.

FIVE FACTS ABOUT THE SERENGETI

1 Much of the Serengeti is legally protected. Located on Tanzania's northern border with Kenya, Serengeti National Park contains 5,700 square miles of grassland plains, savannas and forests. The part of the Serengeti that stretches into Kenya is called Maasai Mara.

2 The Serengeti is home to many animals people think of when they think of Africa, including lions, cheetahs, elephants, rhinos, gazelles, giraffes, hyenas, ostriches, crocodiles, zebras and more.

3 The park is a popular tourist destination, famous for the annual migration of more than a million wildebeests. Along with hundreds of thousands of zebras and gazelles, the grazers travel around 500 miles following the rains in search of fresh grass to graze on.

4 Serengeti comes from the Maasai word *serengit*, which means "endless plains."

5 An active volcano called Ol Doinyo Lengai is in the Serengeti. Its lava eruptions are full of minerals that help make the surrounding grasslands especially fertile, and a favorite place for wildebeests to birth calves during their migration.

AFRICAN ELEPHANT

SCIENTIFIC NAME
Loxodonta africana
LENGTH
8.2 to 13 feet
DIET Herbivore
LOCATION
Central and Southern Africa

In ancient Greek, *loxós* means "slanting" and *odoús* means "tooth."

Elephants are the largest animals on land and can weigh up to an incredible 7 tons—that's 14,000 pounds! Unsurprisingly, they also eat a lot of food, up to 300 pounds per day.

African elephants are very social creatures that live in herds of up to 100. A herd is usually led by the largest and oldest female elephant, known as the matriarch.

TREMENDOUS TRUNK

An elephant's trunk is really a super long nose, but it's also much more than that. Elephants use their trunks to suck up water and spray it down their mouths or over their bodies, to pick up food and even as a snorkel!

Wild But True!

You can tell an African elephant (left) from an Asian one (above) by its ears—African elephant ears are bigger, floppier and shaped like the continent!

AFRICAN WILD DOG

In Greek, this means "painted wolf."

SCIENTIFIC NAME
Lycaon pictus
LENGTH
29.5 to 43 inches
DIET Carnivore
LOCATION
Sub-Saharan
Africa

Like many dogs, African wild dogs live in packs. They are extremely social—the entire pack helps care for the leaders' young, as well as any hurt or sick pack members.

African wild dogs hunt in packs of between six and 20, and often take down large animals like wildebeests and antelopes. If big game is scarce, they will also hunt birds and rodents.

EXTRA LARGE EARS

These pups have giant, rounded ears that they can easily turn, helping them pick up the quietest sounds.

Wild But True!

African wild dogs only have four toes on each paw—most dogs have five toes on their front paws.

AMERICAN BISON

SCIENTIFIC NAME
Bison bison
LENGTH
7 to 11.5 feet
DIET Herbivore
LOCATION
Northwest
U.S.

In Latin, bison means "wild ox."

Weighing up to 2,200 pounds, bison are the heaviest land animals in North America! These massive creatures are also fast for their size, with a top speed of 40 miles per hour. Bison are relatively calm creatures that spend up to 11 hours a day foraging for food. In the winter, bison use their heads like snowplows to push aside snow to get to the grass beneath it.

Wild But True!
*Bison often "wallow,"
or roll in the dirt to help
themselves get rid of fleas
and shed excess fur.*

TELL-TAIL MOOD

When a bison's tail is down
and swinging, it's in a good
mood. If it's standing straight
up, get out of the way—it
might be about to charge.

BABOON

SCIENTIFIC NAME *Papio*
LENGTH 20 to 34 inches
DIET Omnivore
LOCATION
Central and Southern Africa

This name likely comes from the Latin *papa*, meaning "father."

A baboon is a genus of Old World monkeys—there are five different species of baboons, all of which live in Africa and Arabia. Like other Old World monkeys, baboons do not have prehensile tails. They can climb trees but spend much of their time on the ground.

Baboons are very social creatures that live in groups called troops. Hundreds of baboons can live in the same troop!

GROOMING GURU

Baboons will take a break during the hottest part of the day to groom each other, a habit that strengthens social bonds.

Wild But True!

Male baboons are up to twice as large as female baboons.

BALD EAGLE

SCIENTIFIC NAME *Haliaeetus leucocephalus*
LENGTH 3 feet
WINGSPAN 8 feet
DIET Carnivore
LOCATION North America

In Greek, *leukos* means "white" and *kephale* means "head."

Bald eagles are incredible flyers, able to soar nearly 2 miles above the ground. They have excellent eyesight and can spot swimming fish up to a mile away. When swooping down to snag a fish, bald eagles will dive at up to 100 miles per hour. They then sail over the water and pluck the fish out with their feet. When they're not fishing, bald eagles will feed by scavenging carrion or stealing food from other animals.

AMAZING AERIES

Eagles build giant nests called aeries, where they take care of two eggs each year.

Wild But True!

Unlike a lot of other species, female bald eagles are a bit bigger than males.

BLACK RHINOCEROS

SCIENTIFIC NAME
Diceros bicornis
LENGTH
4.5 to 6 feet
DIET Herbivore
LOCATION
Eastern and
Southern Africa

In Latin, *bi* means "two" and *cornis* means "horn."

Black rhinoceroses are very aggressive with somewhat poor eyesight. This combination of traits means they charge at anything they think might be a threat, and sometimes run into trees or rocks.

Despite this embarrassing tendency, rhinos are strong fighters. Humans are their only real threat, as some cultures highly value rhino horns. Both males and females have long horns. Males use them to fight any aggressors they come across, while females use them to protect their young.

Wild But True!

Though their sight is bad, black rhinos have a great sense of smell and can locate each other by scent.

LOOK AT THE LIP

Both black and white rhinos are really gray—the difference is in their upper lips. A black rhino's upper lip is pointed and meant for plucking leaves and fruit, while a white one's (right) is squared for eating grass.

BLACK VULTURE

SCIENTIFIC NAME
Coragyps atratus
LENGTH 2 feet
WINGSPAN 5 feet
DIET Omnivore
LOCATION
North and South
America

Atratus is Latin for "clothed in black."

While black vultures occasionally kill small prey, they are more infamous for mostly eating carrion, which is the flesh of animals that have already died. Black vultures do not have a very good sense of smell, so they sometimes have a hard time finding their next meal. To make up for this, they follow turkey vultures, which can smell carrion from up to a mile away. Once they've been led to a carcass, black vultures will team up to take it from the turkey vulture.

NO NESTS

Instead of building a nest, black vultures lay their eggs (usually two at a time) on the ground of a cave or in a hollow log or tree.

Wild But True!

Black vultures are monogamous—they mate with the same partner for long periods.

BROWN BEAR

SCIENTIFIC NAME *Ursus arctos*
LENGTH 5 to 9 feet
DIET Omnivore
LOCATION Northern Asia, Europe and North America

Ursos (Latin) and arctos (Greek) both mean "bear."

Brown bears are famous for hibernating for four to seven months during the winter. They'll eat up to 90 pounds of food per day in the fall to pack on fat, and can lose up to half their body weight after they have finished hibernating. Female bears without cubs will usually be pregnant when they go into hibernation and give birth midway through. The mother's cubs will nurse on her milk until the following spring, and stay with their mother for the next two and a half years.

Wild But True!

A group of brown bears is called a sloth or a sleuth.

SURPRISING SPEED

Brown bears can weigh up to 700 pounds and run at a top speed of 30 miles per hour.

BURROWING OWL

SCIENTIFIC NAME
Athene cunicularia
LENGTH 10 inches
WINGSPAN 20 to
24 inches
DIET Carnivore
LOCATION
North and South
America

These owls are named for Athena, the Greek goddess of wisdom.

Burrowing owls are a bit unusual. They hunt during the day and night, and unlike many other birds, they spend much of their time on the ground. In fact, they nest in the ground, too! Most of the time, they don't dig the holes themselves, though. Instead, they steal holes that have been made by other burrowing animals, like prairie dogs.

Wild But True!

When they get scared, burrowing owls make a hissing sound similar to a rattlesnake.

BAIT AND WAIT

These owls will sometimes put animal dung outside their burrow—scientists think this is done to attract bugs, which the owl can then eat.

CARACAL

SCIENTIFIC NAME
Caracal caracal
LENGTH 3 feet
DIET Carnivore
LOCATION
Africa and
Southern Asia

The name caracal has Turkish roots, from *kara* ("black") and *kulak* ("ear").

This wild cat has extremely strong hind legs, enabling it to jump 6 feet up in the air—perfect for snatching a bird before it's able to fly away.

Caracals keep their claws sharp by dragging them on trees, an action that simultaneously marks their territory since these cats have scent glands between their toes.

TALL TUFTS

Scientists think caracals twitch the tufts of hair on their ears to communicate, and that they may also help these wild cats hear more clearly.

Wild But True!

A caracal's footpads are covered with stiff fur, making them super silent as they stalk their prey.

CHEETAH

SCIENTIFIC NAME
Acinonyx jubatus
LENGTH 6 to 8 feet
DIET Carnivore
LOCATION
Africa

In Greek, *akinētos* means "motionless."

Before it sprints off to catch its next meal, a cheetah can stay amazingly still and silent. Its spots make it hard to pick out in tall grass and its eyes let this predator see very well.

Cheetahs are famous for being the fastest mammals on land, reaching speeds of up to 70 miles per hour. However, the cheetah can only run this fast for about 300 yards. If it is successful in catching something, it needs to wait about half an hour to catch its breath before eating.

Wild But True!

A cheetah has smaller teeth in comparison to other big cats. This leaves room for larger nasal passages and allows for quicker breathing—one of the things they need to run so fast!

IDENTIFYING MARKS

You can tell a leopard (above) apart from a cheetah by looking at its face. Cheetahs have black tear marks running from inside their eyes down around their mouths.

81

GIRAFFE

Giraffes are named after camels for their long necks and leopards (*pardalis* in Greek) for their spots.

SCIENTIFIC NAME
Giraffa camelopardalis
LENGTH 14 to 19 feet
DIET Herbivore
LOCATION Africa

Giraffes spend most of their day eating up to 100 pounds of food. They even eat leaves from thorny trees that deter most predators. Giraffes use their super long tongues and prehensile lips to eat around the thorns. If they accidentally swallow one, it's OK—they have very thick, sticky saliva that coats the thorn.

When they're not eating, they stay on the lookout for predators. While their height usually protects them from predators, adult giraffes are vulnerable to lion or crocodile attacks when they're sleeping or drinking water. To stay safe, they often do these tasks in shifts. If forced, a giraffe will defend itself with a deadly kick.

QUICK NAPPER

Giraffes need shockingly little sleep—less than half an hour per day! They get this by taking 2-minute naps throughout the day.

HIPPOPOTAMUS

SCIENTIFIC NAME
Hippopotamus amphibious
LENGTH 12 to 15 feet
DIET Herbivore
LOCATION Africa

This name comes from the Greek hippos potamios, which translates to "river horse."

Hippopotamuses beat the heat by spending most of their time underwater—they swim around or simply stand in rivers for up to 16 hours per day and leave the water at night to graze on the nearby grasses for food. Hippos are known to travel around 6 miles per night, enabling them to eat about 80 pounds of grass!

When hippos do sunbathe, their skin is naturally protected by an oily red substance that they secrete.

UNDERWATER EXPERT

When a hippo is completely submerged, its nose and ears automatically close to keep water out.

Wild But True!

A hippo calf is born weighing 100 pounds.

LION

SCIENTIFIC NAME
Panthera leo
LENGTH 4.5 to 6.5 feet
DIET Carnivore
LOCATION Africa

In Greek, *pan* means "all" and *thēr* means "beast of prey."

In a pride of lions, one or two males protect the territory—their thick manes help protect their necks if they need to fight with another lion. Meanwhile, it is the female lions' job to do the hunting. Because they are not faster than most other animals they are chasing, lionesses rely on teamwork to surround and attack their prey.

Lion cubs do not help with the hunting until they are about a year old. When male lions reach adulthood, they leave and attempt to take over another lion's pride.

FAR-RANGING ROAR

A male lion's roar can be heard up to 5 miles away. It's mostly used to warn off other animals and call members of the pride back home.

NAKED MOLE RAT

SCIENTIFIC NAME
Heterocephalus glaber
LENGTH 3 to 13 inches
DIET Herbivore
LOCATION Eastern Africa

Glaber is the Latin word for "bald."

With their hairless, wrinkled bodies and giant buck teeth, naked mole rats are very unusual-looking creatures. They live together in large groups in underground burrows and hardly ever go above ground.

Like ants or bees, naked mole rats live in eusocial colonies. This means they structure their community around one dominant female, known as the queen. Worker rats build their burrows and gather roots and bulbs for the whole colony to eat, while other rats look after the queen.

BLIND AS A RAT

Naked mole rats have no external ears and tiny eyes, so they are mostly blind. They rely on their sense of smell and feeling vibrations and air currents.

Wild But True!

Unlike most mammals, naked mole rats cannot regulate their own body temperatures and must huddle together or rest in tunnels near the surface for warmth.

NINE-BANDED ARMADILLO

SCIENTIFIC NAME
Dasypus novemcinctus
LENGTH 2.5 feet
DIET Omnivore
LOCATION Southeastern
United States

In Latin, *novem* means "nine" and *cinctus* means "band."

While they do eat a little bit of plants to round out their diet, nine-banded armadillos are mostly insectivores—they love eating bugs! These mostly nocturnal creatures spend much of the night and early morning using their noses to dig through loose soil and munching on any insects they find.

If the nine-banded armadillo gets startled by another creature, it literally jumps in fright. These small mammals can leap 3 to 4 feet in the air, which is often surprising enough to send any predators running.

AWESOME ARMOR

An armadillo has outer body "armor" made up of bony plates covered in tough skin, giving them a tough but flexible exterior. Many have exactly nine bands, but it can range from seven to 11.

Wild But True!

A nine-banded armadillo can hold its breath for up to 6 minutes and is known to cross narrow bodies of water by simply walking along the bottom.

OSTRICH

SCIENTIFIC NAME
Struthio camelus
LENGTH 7
to 9 feet
DIET Omnivore
LOCATION
Africa

In Latin,
struthio
means
" ostrich. "

W eighing up to 350 pounds, it's not
surprising that ostriches cannot fly.
But they can still move very quickly,
sprinting at up to 43 miles per hour. Their wings
also help them while they're running, acting like
rudders to help them change direction.

Ostriches also use their wings for courtship and
for communication. Lifted wings and tail feathers
convey dominance, while letting the wings and
tail hang downward shows submission.

INCREDIBLE KICK

An ostrich's long, strong legs can deliver kicks powerful enough to kill a lion.

PRAIRIE DOG

SCIENTIFIC NAME
Cynomys
LENGTH 12 to 15 inches
DIET Herbivore
LOCATION North American

This comes from the Greek words for "dog" and "mouse."

Prairie dogs are expert tunnelers, building extensive underground homes that have designated sections for toilets, sleeping and even nurseries.
Most prairie dog tunnels cover less than half a square mile, but the largest known system covered more than 25,000 square miles.
Though they spend much of their time in these tunnels, prairie dogs do emerge to forage for food. Because they mostly eat grass, which provides all the moisture they need, prairie dogs don't need to drink water directly.

FAMILY FIRST

Prairie dogs are all about group living—they share food, groom one another and say hello by touching noses.

Wild But True!

Prairie dogs got their name because of their dog-like bark.

PRAIRIE RATTLESNAKE

Crotalus comes from the Greek krotalon, which means rattle.

SCIENTIFIC NAME
Crotalus viridis
LENGTH 3 to 4 feet
DIET Carnivore
LOCATION
Western
North America

SUPER SMELLER

The prairie rattlesnake has an excellent sense of smell, using both its nostrils and forked tongue to pick up on scents.

Like all rattlesnakes, the prairie rattlesnake is a kind of pit viper. Pit vipers are named for the pits, or hollows, located on their heads between their nostrils and eyes, which are the openings to extremely sensitive heat-sensing organs used to find prey.

Being a viper means the prairie rattlesnake also has hollow, venom-filled retractable fangs, which it uses on its prey. This snake mostly eats small mammals, but will prey on just about anything it can find, including small birds, amphibians and even other snakes.

Wild But True!

Every time a rattlesnake sheds its skin, another segment is added to the rattle on its tail.

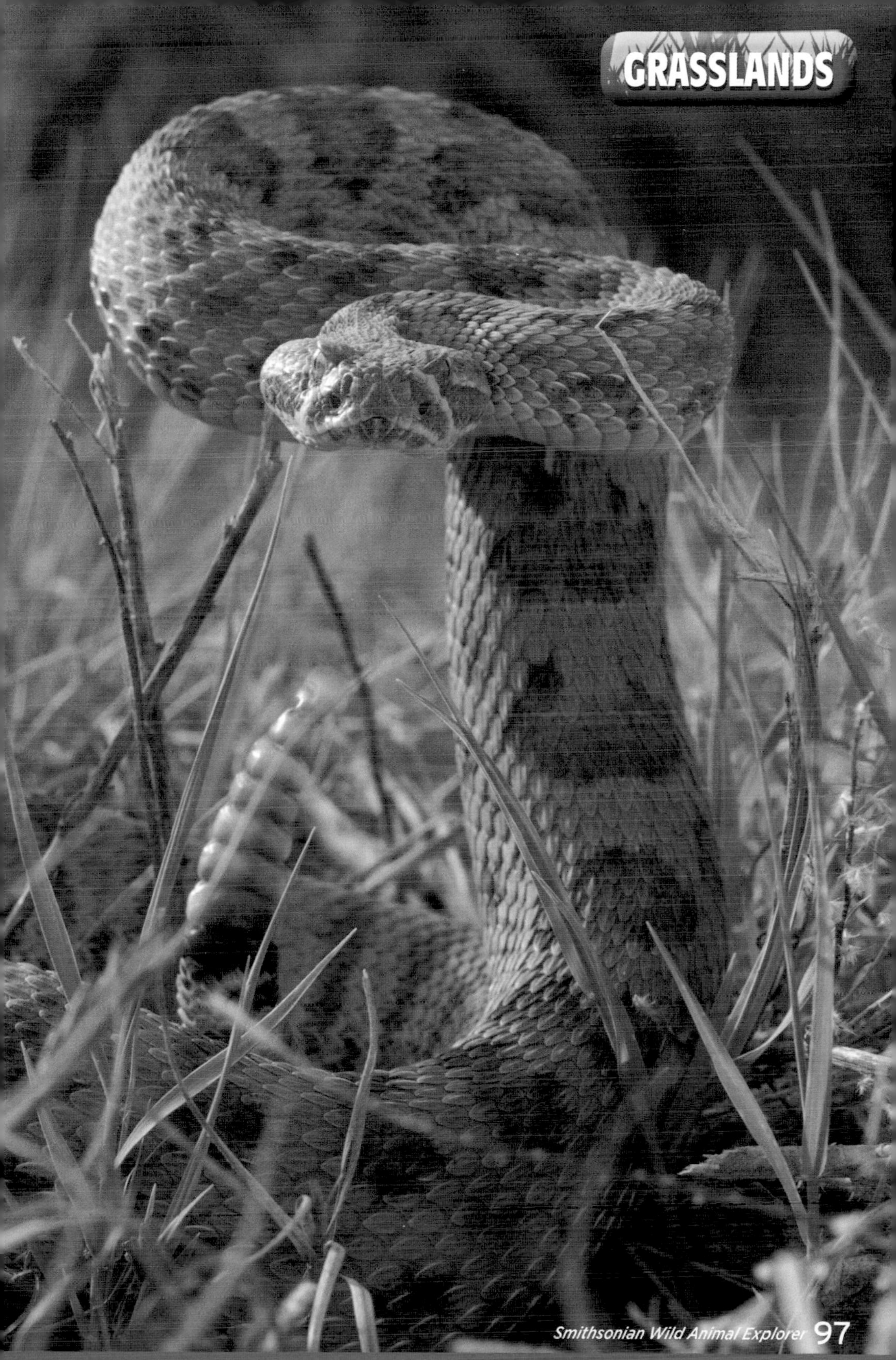

RED KANGAROO

In Greek, *makros* means "long," and *pous* means "foot."

SCIENTIFIC NAME *Macropus rufus*
LENGTH 3 to 6 feet
DIET Herbivore
LOCATION Australia

At about 200 pounds, kangaroos are the world's largest marsupials. Like all other marsupials, kangaroos are born before they are fully developed and finish growing in their mother's pouch. Kangaroos will emerge at around 2 months, but won't leave their mother's pouch for good until they're 8 to 10 months old.

Kangaroos are also known for their extremely strong legs. These giant marsupials can reach speeds of up to 35 miles per hour and clear about 25 feet in a single leap. While male kangaroos are bigger and stronger, females are lighter and faster.

KANGAROO KICKS

Though kangaroos only eat plants, they're still excellent fighters. When fighting over a mate, male kangaroos will lean back on their tails and "box" with their competitor by kicking their feet.

Wild But True!

A baby kangaroo is called a joey, and a group of kangaroos is called a mob.

SKUNK

SCIENTIFIC NAME
Mephitis mephitis
LENGTH 8 to 19 inches
DIET Omnivore
LOCATION North and South Africa

Mephitis also means "a foul smelling odor."

When a skunk feels threatened, it will stamp its feet, lift its tail and growl. This is every other animal's cue to leave unless they want to get hit with the skunk's seriously smelly spray, also known as "musk." A skunk can spray its musk up to 12 feet away, and often aims for its attacker's eyes. This defense is extremely effective except on some animals like the great horned owl, which doesn't have a very good sense of smell.

Wild But True!
If you get sprayed by a skunk, you'll have a hard time getting rid of the smell for a couple of days.

HONEY LOVER

Skunks are known to attack bee hives—they like to eat the honey bees.

SPOTTED HYENA

SCIENTIFIC NAME
Crocuta crocuta
LENGTH 34
to 59 inches
DIET Omnivore
LOCATION
Africa

From the Greek *krokottas*, which means "a wild animal."

Hyenas live in groups called clans. A clan may have up to 80 hyenas, and females are always in charge. Female hyenas are also known as some of the most devoted animal mothers.

Hyenas are known for being scavengers, but they can also take down larger prey like antelope. They hunt in packs and work together to get a herd animal on its own, but teamwork goes out the window once their prey is taken down—hyenas often fight over the food they've just earned.

ADVENTUROUS EATER

Hyenas eat just about everything—even the bones of their prey. Their strong teeth can crunch them up, allowing hyenas to digest what they can and excrete the extra calcium.

Wild But True!

Though hyenas look similar to dogs, they are more closely related to cats.

THOMSON'S GAZELLE

SCIENTIFIC NAME
Eudorcas thomsonii
LENGTH 20 to 43 inches
DIET Herbivore
LOCATION East Africa

This gazelle is named for Scottish explorer Joseph Thomson.

Wild But True!

Thomson's gazelles live in drier grasslands and will regularly travel long distances to get a drink of water.

SUDDEN SPEED

Standing out in the open makes them vulnerable to predators, but the gazelle is pretty fast, moving at speeds of up to 40 miles per hour.

A member of the antelope family, the Thomson's gazelle spends much of its time grazing on grass, shoots and leaves. They're especially well-known for their impressive ringed horns, which can grow up to 17 inches.

Like other gazelles, this mammal does a special jump known as "pronking," which involves repeatedly jumping up and down with straight legs and a curved back. Scientists aren't sure why gazelles engage in pronking, but it's thought to be their way of showing off athleticism and energy—with any luck, potential predators will decide not to bother and look for weaker prey.

TIGER

SCIENTIFIC NAME
Panthera tigris
LENGTH 6 feet
DIET Carnivore
LOCATION Asia

Tigris is Greek for "arrow."

Tigers are the largest wild cats in the world, weighing more than 700 pounds. They're excellent hunters, usually taking down large prey like deer or antelope, and prefer to hunt at night. Because tigers can't finish eating all that meat at once, they'll cover any leftovers with leaves and dirt and return to it for another meal the following night.

Despite their size, tigers can also move very quickly, up to 40 miles per hour. They keep their balance with the help of their tail. Their tail has a secondary purpose, too—communication! When aggressive, a tiger will lash its tail from side to side. An investigating tiger holds its tail high, and a nervous one will keep it low.

SPECIAL STRIPES

A tiger's stripes help it camouflage itself in long grass. No two tigers have the same set of stripes—each tiger's pattern is unique. It's also not just their fur that has stripes. Tigers also have striped skin!

Wild But True!

Unlike most cats, tigers enjoy the water and are excellent swimmers.

WARTHOG

SCIENTIFIC NAME
Phacochoerus africanus
LENGTH
30 inches
DIET Herbivore
LOCATION
Africa

In Ancient Greek, *phakos* means "lens" and *choiros* means "pig."

Though they look pretty wild, warthogs are closely related to domestic pigs. They spend most of their day grazing or rooting around for roots or bulbs to munch on, and can go for up to several months without water in the dry seasons.

Like their pig cousins, warthogs also enjoy taking mud baths when the opportunity arises. The mud helps them cool down and protects them from insects—something that can be especially bothersome for a creature that is mostly bald.

FLIGHT BEFORE FIGHT

Though they look tough, most warthogs will choose to run when confronted by a predator. If cornered, they will attack with their tusks.

Wild But True!

Warthogs are named for the "warts," or protective bumps, that cover their heads.

WILD TURKEY

SCIENTIFIC NAME
Meleagris gallopavo

LENGTH
3.6 to 3.8 feet

WINGSPAN
4.1 to 4.8 feet

DIET Omnivore

LOCATION
North America

In Latin, *gallus* means "chicken" and *pāvō* means "peacock."

Wild turkeys were almost completely wiped out in the early 1900s due to overhunting and loss of their habitat to settlers. In the 1940s, Americans decided to relocate the birds to areas with plenty of woodlands and their population has greatly recovered.

Though we think of turkeys having ruffled feathers, a big tail and bald head, it's only the male turkeys that display these traits. Females are quite dark and plain in comparison and also lack the male's signature beard.

Wild But True!

Benjamin Franklin did not want the bald eagle to be the national bird—instead, he lobbied for the wild turkey.

SURPRISING SPEED

Wild turkeys can sprint at 25 miles per hour and fly at 55 miles per hour.

ZEBRA

SCIENTIFIC NAME
Equus quagga
LENGTH
3.5 to 5 feet
DIET Herbivore
LOCATION
Africa

The quagga was a now-extinct cousin of the zebra.

Famous for their stripes, zebras spend most of their time with the rest of their herd, grazing on the plains of Africa. Scientists aren't sure why these animals have stripes, though they have a few theories. One is that when they stand together as a herd, the stripes make it difficult for other animals to pick out any one zebra. Another is that the stripes help them regulate body heat, as the darker patches absorb more of the sun's rays than the lighter ones.

TREMENDOUS TEETH

A zebra's teeth never actually stop growing! They're just constantly being filed down by all the chewing they do.

Wild But True!

Every zebra's stripe pattern is unique, just like a person's fingerprint.

113

QUICK QUIZ

ARE YOU A GRASSLANDS EXPERT?

1 How can you tell an African elephant from an Asian elephant?
   A. Look at its trunk.
   B. Look at its tail.
   C. Look at its ears.

2 What are brown bears famous for doing during the winter?
   A. Hunting
   B. Hibernating
   C. Climbing

3 In a pride of lions, who does the hunting?
   A. The male
   B. The females
   C. They hunt together

4 Can ostriches fly?
   A. Nope!
   B. Just a little.
   C. Yes, really well.

5 Why do warthogs take mud baths?
   A. It keeps them cool.
   B. It prevents bugs from biting them.
   C. A and B

6 How far can a skunk spray its musk?
   A. 2 feet
   B. 12 feet
   C. 20 feet

JOKE CORNER

GRASSLAND GUFFAWS

What did the buffalo say to his boy as he left for school?
Bison!

What do you call bears with no ears?
B!

What does a lion say when she meets another animal?
Pleased to eat you!

What is black and white and red all over?
A sunburned zebra!

What type of key won't open any door?
A turkey!

What do you call brown bears when they're caught in the rain?
Drizzly bears!

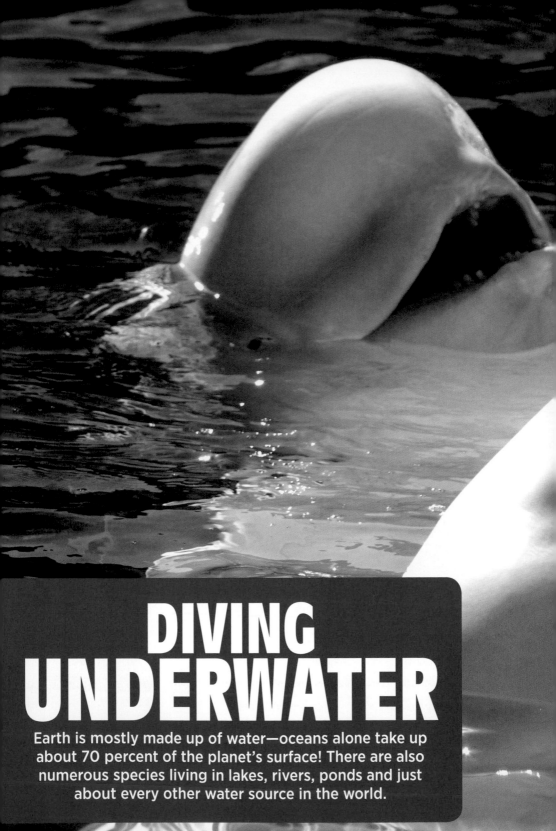

DIVING
UNDERWATER

Earth is mostly made up of water—oceans alone take up about 70 percent of the planet's surface! There are also numerous species living in lakes, rivers, ponds and just about every other water source in the world.

AROUND THE

Atlantic
Ocean

Pacific
Ocean

Lots of Layers

The ocean has three different layers. Most animals, like sea turtles and dolphins, live in the surface layer, where the sunlight keeps the waters warmer and lets plants grow. Below this is the twilight zone, which gets filtered light and has animals with bigger eyes, like squids. At the very bottom is the deep ocean, which is pitch black and has some of the most unusual creatures, like giant spider crabs.

WORLD

Arctic
Ocean

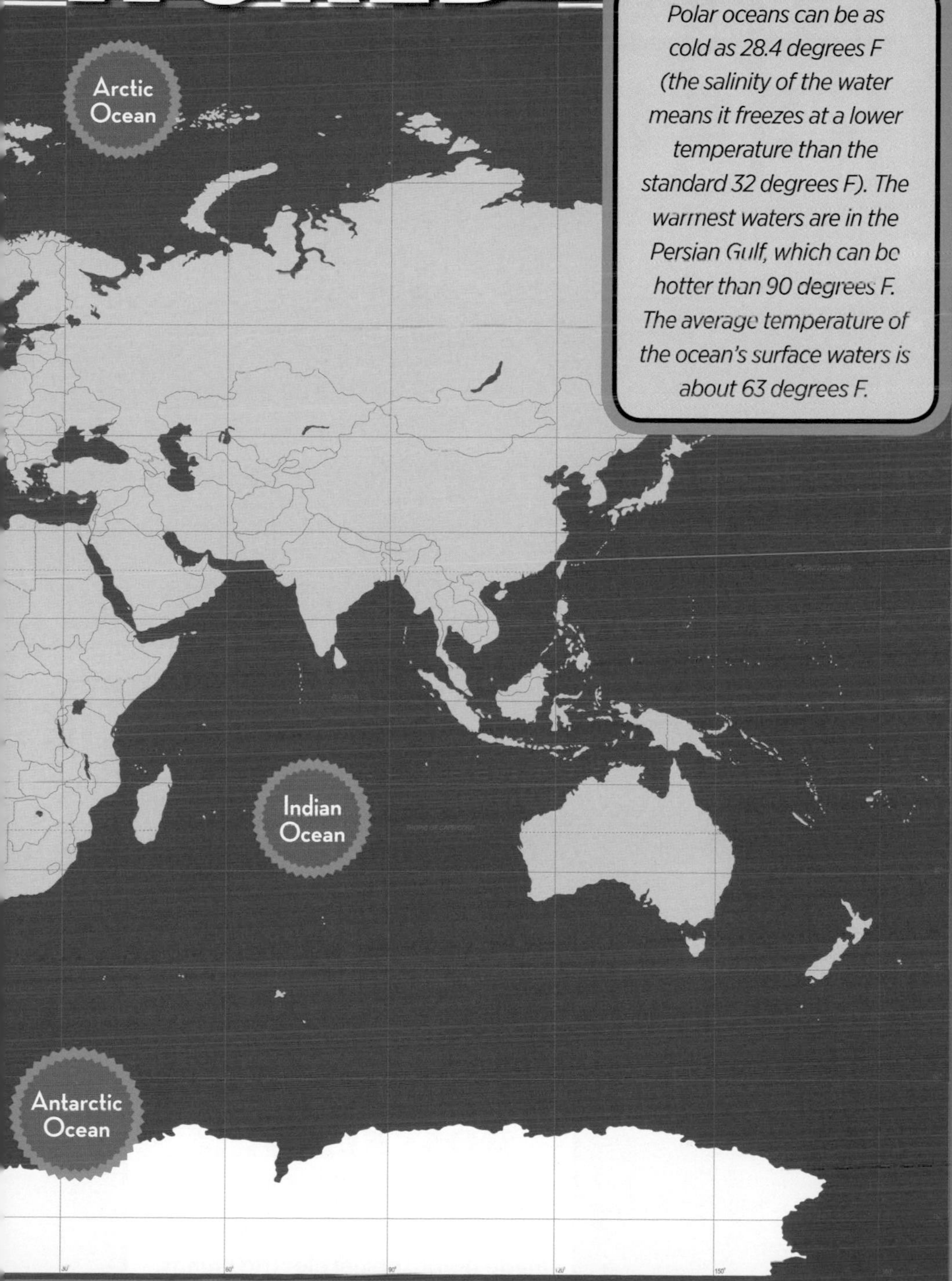

Polar oceans can be as
cold as 28.4 degrees F
(the salinity of the water
means it freezes at a lower
temperature than the
standard 32 degrees F). The
warmest waters are in the
Persian Gulf, which can be
hotter than 90 degrees F.
The average temperature of
the ocean's surface waters is
about 63 degrees F.

Indian
Ocean

Antarctic
Ocean

WILD WORLD RECORDS

BECAUSE THEIR SKELETONS (IF THEY EVEN HAVE THEM) DON'T NEED TO SUPPORT AS MUCH WEIGHT UNDERWATER, SEA CREATURES CAN GET MUCH BIGGER THAN LAND ANIMALS.

SMARTEST CREATURE IN THE SEA
OCTOPUS

It's difficult to measure intelligence, but octopuses have been known to make tools out of shells, solve mazes and open jars.

MOST ELECTRIC
ELECTRIC EEL

Eighty percent of their bodies are made up of special electric organs.

TOOTHIEST GRIN
GREAT WHITE SHARK
Great whites have rows and rows of about 300 serrated teeth!

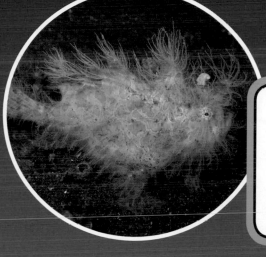

WEIRDEST WALKER
HAIRY FROGFISH
Even though it doesn't have feet, this fish "walks" along the ocean floor with its fins.

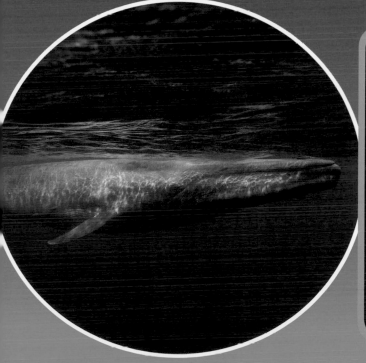

BIGGEST ANIMAL EVER ON EARTH
BLUE WHALE
Weighing up to 400,000 pounds and stretching a jaw-dropping 100 feet, no one's ever seen evidence of a heavier animal than the blue whale.

FIVE FACTS ABOUT THE GREAT BARRIER REEF

LOCATED IN THE CORAL SEA OFF THE COAST OF QUEENSLAND, AUSTRALIA, THE GREAT BARRIER REEF IS THE LARGEST LIVING STRUCTURE IN THE WORLD.

2 The Great Barrier Reef is about 1,429 miles long. That's roughly the distance from Maine to Florida!

1 Coral are animals that look a lot like plants. Young coral buds, or polyps, attach themselves to other coral polyps, creating colonies called reefs.

3 The Reef has existed for about 500,000 years, but the current structure is about 6-8,000 years old.

4 Astronauts can see the Great Barrier Reef from outer space.

5 Lots of animals call this coral reef home, including fish, sea turtles, clams, seahorses, stingrays, sharks and more.

BELUGA WHALE

SCIENTIFIC NAME
Delphinapterus leucas

LENGTH
13 to 20 feet

DIET Carnivore

LOCATION
Arctic Coast

In Greek, *delphis* means "dolphin" and *apterus* means "without wing."

B elugas are one of the smallest species of whales. They're still pretty large though, weighing up to 1.5 tons. Belugas are easily recognized by their rounded foreheads and lack of dorsal fins.

Like many whales, belugas use echolocation to navigate underwater. Belugas make clicking sounds that travel through the water and bounce back to them—it's an especially useful trick for finding breathing holes in the ice. Their curved foreheads, known as melons, help to focus the sound waves as they project them.

COOL AS ICE

Belugas are also called white whales. Their pale skin helps them blend in with ice, hiding them from predators like polar bears.

Wild But True!

Beluga whales are born gray or brown, and fade to white by the time they're 5 years old.

BLUE MARLIN

SCIENTIFIC NAME
Makaira nigricans
LENGTH
11 to 14 feet
DIET Carnivore
LOCATION
Temperate Oceans

In Greek, machaira means "short sword" or "bent dagger."

Wild But True!

Female blue marlins are much bigger than males. Most marlins weigh 200 to 400 pounds, but some can weigh up to almost 2,000 pounds!

SUPER SPEAR

Blue marlins put their spears to good use. They purposefully swim through crowded schools of fish and then circle back to prey on those that were wounded by their upper jaw.

Blue marlins are migratory fish that have been recorded swimming more than 4,500 nautical miles—one blue marlin was tagged off the east coast of the United States and picked up again in the Indian Ocean.

Though they are cold-blooded like other fish, blue marlins do have the ability to regulate their eye and brain temperatures, keeping them warm. This improves eyesight and thinking, giving blue marlins a big advantage when hunting.

BLUE WHALE

SCIENTIFIC NAME
Balaenoptera musculus
LENGTH 82 to 105 feet
DIET Carnivore
LOCATION Oceans

Musculus is Latin for "little mouse."

Weighing up to an incredible 200 tons—that's 400,000 pounds—blue whales are the largest animals to have ever lived on Earth (that we know of).

Blue whales mostly feed on small crustaceans called krill. The whales take an enormous gulp of water, then use their tongues to strain it out between fringed plates of baleen (a fingernail-like material) attached to their jaws. Thousands of krill are left behind, which the whale then swallows.

Wild But True!

Blue whales are some of the loudest animals on the planet. They communicate with moans and groans that scientists think other blue whales can hear up to 1,000 miles away.

BIG BABY

Newborn blue whales already weigh 3 tons and are about 25 feet long. They grow rapidly, gaining about 200 pounds each day while feeding on their mother's milk.

BLUE-SPOTTED RIBBONTAIL RAY

SCIENTIFIC NAME
Taeniura lymma
LENGTH
12 to 14 inches
DIET Carnivore
LOCATION
Indo-Pacific Ocean

Taenia is Latin for "stripe" and oura is Greek for "tail."

The blue-spotted ribbontail is a kind of stingray that likes to bury itself at the sandy bottom of a coral reef, where it waits for its next meal. This stingray has a special skill called electroreception—that means it can detect the electrical fields being emitted from the other fish around it. When the blue-spotted ribbontail senses some prey, it scoops it up for a snack.

Blue-spotted stingrays mostly live alone or in small groups. When they are together, they may also use electroreception to communicate with one another.

TOUCHY TAIL

The end of this stingray's ribbon-like tail has two spines, which it uses to attack when necessary.

Wild But True!

Blue-spotted ribbontails have strong plates in their mouths, which they use for crushing the hard shells of mollusks, crabs and prawns.

BOTTLENOSE DOLPHIN

SCIENTIFIC NAME
Tursiops truncatus
LENGTH
10 to 14 feet
DIET Carnivore
LOCATION
Temperate oceans

Truncatus is Latin for "shortened."

K nown for being playful and intelligent, bottlenose dolphins are incredible communicators. They "talk" to each other not only by using various squeaks and whistles, but also with all kinds of body language, from jumping to slapping their tails to butting heads.

Dolphins also use their voices another way: They emit high-frequency clicking noises and use echolocation to determine the size, shape, speed and location of objects or other animals that are far away.

Wild But True!
Each dolphin has a special whistle it uses to identify itself, similar to how humans have names.

FRIENDS FOR LIFE

Dolphins are extremely social creatures that can live for up to 50 years and are known to spend decades playing, hunting and mating with the same group.

BOX JELLYFISH

SCIENTIFIC NAME
Cubozoa
LENGTH 10 feet
DIET Carnivore
LOCATION
Waters off
Northern Australia
and throughout the
Indo-Pacific

This class name refers to the cube-like shape of their bells.

Jellyfish are invertebrates, which means they lack a backbone or bony skeleton. Unlike other kinds of jellyfish, which can only drift, box jellyfish are able to move purposefully through the water at up to 4 knots.

Box jellyfish have up to 15 tentacles, each up to 10 feet long, growing from each corner of their bells. They use the tentacles to bring food up to their mouths. Once they are finished digesting, the jellyfish will expel waste from that same opening.

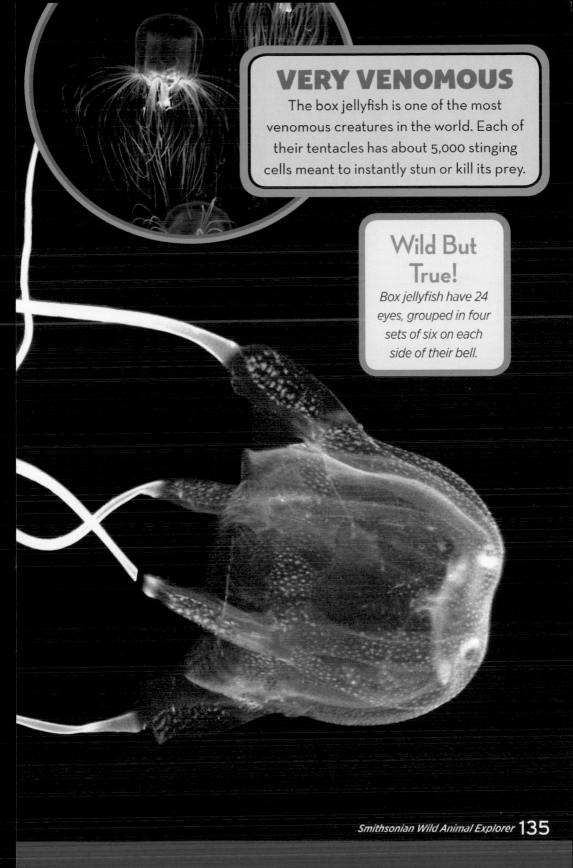

VERY VENOMOUS

The box jellyfish is one of the most venomous creatures in the world. Each of their tentacles has about 5,000 stinging cells meant to instantly stun or kill its prey.

Wild But True!

Box jellyfish have 24 eyes, grouped in four sets of six on each side of their bell.

CALIFORNIA SEA LION

SCIENTIFIC NAME
Zalophus californianus
LENGTH 5.5 to 7.5 feet
DIET Carnivore
LOCATION North America's West Coast

Zalophus means "with crest" in Latin, a reference to the adult male sea lion's crested skull.

The California sea lion is a semi-aquatic mammal that usually swims in open waters, where they hunt for their favorite foods, including fish, squid and shellfish. However, thanks to their forward-rotating rear flippers, they can move pretty well on land, too!

California sea lions are very social animals. When they're not hunting (something they can do for up to 30 hours at a time!), they're often hanging out in groups, sometimes floating all together in "rafts." They are also known to "porpoise," or leap out of the water while swimming, which likely increases their speed.

Wild But True!

California sea lions are the fastest species of sea lion, swimming at a top speed of 25 miles per hour.

DEEP DIVE

For an animal that can't breathe underwater, California sea lions sure can dive! This mammal can reach depths of up to 900 feet and stay underwater for up to 10 minutes, a trick it pulls off by lowering its heart rate.

CARIBBEAN REEF SHARK

From its profile, it looks as though the Caribbean reef shark has a pointed nose, but from below you can see it's actually quite rounded. The reef shark's upper body is dark gray or gray-brown, with a yellow or white underside.

Like many other sharks, the Caribbean reef shark mostly eats bony fish. On top of having excellent sight, smell and hearing, Caribbean reef sharks can detect vibrations in the water and low-frequency sounds, which are usually made by a struggling nearby fish.

SCIENTIFIC NAME
Carcharhinus perezi
LENGTH 5 to 10 feet
DIET Carnivore
LOCATION Caribbean waters

In Greek, *kacharos* means "sharpen" and *rhinos* means "nose."

PARASITE PARADISE

Caribbean reef sharks are regular hosts to parasites, often hosting dark leeches on their dorsal fins.

Wild But True!

Scientists have observed these sharks "sleeping" in caves and on the ocean floor but have no explanation for this behavior.

DUCK-BILLED PLATYPUS

SCIENTIFIC NAME
Ornithorhynchus anatinus
LENGTH 1.5 feet
DIET Carnivore
LOCATION Australia's East Coast

Anatinus means "duck-like" in Latin.

Duck-billed platypuses are small creatures that like to spend much of their time swimming and hunting in freshwater. To swim, they use their front feet to paddle, and their back feet and tail to shift directions.

These mammals use their super-sensitive noses to detect insects, shellfish and worms from the sandy bottoms of shallow waters. Duck-billed platypuses don't have teeth, so they also pick up a little bit of gravel with their meals to help them chew it.

QUITE A KICK

The bottoms of this platypus's back feet have venomous stingers, helping protect them from any creature that attacks from behind.

Wild But True!

Duck-billed platypuses are made for the water, with flat heads and bodies perfect for gliding; thick fur that lets them stay warm and dry, even after hours of swimming; and nostrils on the top of their bills, letting them breathe while floating.

ELECTRIC EEL

SCIENTIFIC NAME
Electrophorus electricus
LENGTH 6 to 8 feet
DIET Carnivore
LOCATION Freshwaters of Northern South America

Phorus is Latin for "bearer of."

Special electric organs make up most of this creature's body. Electric eels send out electric pulses to do just about everything: to hunt, to defend themselves, to navigate and even to communicate. They can send out shocks of varying strength, the strongest being about 600 volts.

Surprisingly, electric eels can even attack land animals—at least, very briefly. If a predator steps into the water, the electric eel will jump up and press its body against the predator so it can deliver a painful shock.

Wild But True!

Technically, electric eels aren't eels, they're just eel-shaped. They are actually more closely related to catfish and carp.

MOUTH BREATHER

Like most fish, electric eels have gills. But unlike other fish, gills aren't the main source of their oxygen, partially because they live in poorly oxygenated waters. Instead, they take in air through their mouths and must regularly come to the surface in order to breathe.

143

FIN WHALE

SCIENTIFIC NAME
Balaenoptera physalus
LENGTH 65 to 85 feet
DIET Carnivore
LOCATION Oceans

In Greek, *physa* means "blows."

Wild But True!

Fin whales are closely related to blue whales and can mate with them—scientists have documented some hybrids in the wild.

SPEEDY SWIMMER

Though slower than many other sea creatures, fin whales are one of the fastest great whales, moving at around 23 miles per hour.

Fin whales are the second-largest species of whale. It's easy to pick one out by its single fin located on the back, close to the tail. They filter-feed in the same way as other baleen whales, taking in very large amounts of krill and pushing out the excess water between their "teeth." Fin whales fast during the winter while they migrate to warmer waters, but during the summer, they'll eat up to 2 tons of krill each day.

145

FLAMINGO

SCIENTIFIC NAME *Phoenicopterus*
LENGTH 2.6 to 4.7 feet
WINGSPAN 3 to 5 feet
DIET Omnivore
LOCATION South America, Africa

In Greek, this means "blood red-feathered."

With their bright pink color, propensity for standing on one leg and the ability to "run" on water with their webbed feet in order to build up speed before taking flight, flamingos are very fascinating birds!

Flamingos always live in groups, though their numbers can vary from a few pairs to tens of thousands. They communicate through physical displays, which are often used to show off for potential mates, and through a lot of different growls, gabbles and honks.

YOU ARE WHAT YOU EAT

Flamingos are so brightly colored because their diet of algae and crustaceans contains a lot of carotenoids, a sort of color pigment.

Wild But True!

Flamingos have a good sense of hearing, but little to no sense of smell.

GIANT PACIFIC OCTOPUS

SCIENTIFIC NAME
Enteroctopus dofleini

LENGTH
9.75 to 16 feet

DIET Carnivore

LOCATION
Northern Pacific

Octopus is Greek for "eight-foot."

G iant Pacific octopuses (or, if you prefer, octopodes) are highly intelligent creatures, shown to be capable of learning how to open jars, solve mazes and mimic other octopuses.

These cephalopods like to hunt at night, mostly on smaller creatures like shrimp, fish and lobsters. However, giant Pacific octopuses have also been known to eat birds and take down larger prey like sharks by using their beak-like mouths to tear at their flesh.

COOL CAMOUFLAGE

Giant octopuses are reddish-brown but have a special color-changing pigment in their skin, enabling them to seamlessly imitate other patterns and blend into the surrounding coral, algae or rocks.

Wild But True!

The record for largest giant Pacific octopus is a whopping 30 feet across with a weight of 600 pounds.

GIANT JAPANESE SPIDER CRAB

Wild But True!

A giant Japanese spider crab is extremely adaptable and can survive easily if it loses a leg—or even three.

These incredibly long-legged crabs also have extremely long lifetimes—scientists believe they can crawl around the ocean floor for up to 100 years, and maybe more. These crabs only get bigger as they age, molting their old exoskeletons and growing new ones.

These crabs will eat just about anything smaller than they are, though they prefer scavenging to hunting and would never pass up any dead creatures that may be floating by.

SCIENTIFIC NAME
Macrocheira kaempferi
LENGTH Up to 15 feet
DIET Omnivore
LOCATION Pacific Ocean near Japan

In Greek, makros means "big" and cheir means "arms."

CLEVER CAMOUFLAGE

This crab's exoskeleton gives it a lot of protection, but it still likes to fade into the rocky ocean floor to stay safe. To further the illusion, spider crabs will cover themselves with sponges and other small creatures.

GREAT WHITE SHARK

SCIENTIFIC NAME
Carcharodon carcharias
LENGTH
15 to 20+ feet
DIET Carnivore
LOCATION
Temperate Oceans

In Greek, *karcharos* means "sharpen" and *odous* means "teeth."

Great white sharks have a reputation for being the perfect predator, and it's easy to see why: they're the largest predatory fish in the world! They can also swim at an impressive 15 miles per hour and have an incredible sense of smell, with the ability to detect a single drop of blood in 25 gallons of water.

Sharks are even able to detect the very small electromagnetic fields given off by other animals. They use all these senses and weapons (and all their teeth) to prey on sea lions and seals, their favorite meals.

Wild But True!

Scientists think that great whites like to "sample bite" humans, which is why so many shark attacks are not fatal. Lucky us!

TONS OF TEETH

Sharks have about 300 serrated teeth, but they don't chew their food—they just use them to tear off chunks of flesh and then swallow them whole.

GREEN SEA TURTLE

SCIENTIFIC NAME
Chelonia mydas
LENGTH Up to 5 feet
DIET Herbivore
LOCATION Temperate Oceans

In Greek, *mydos* means "wetness."

Sea turtles are famous for coming to shore in order to lay eggs, which they bury in the sand. The eggs hatch about two months later. They are immediately in danger as predators try to snatch them up before the tiny turtles can make it to the water.

These turtles are so dedicated to their beaches that they'll travel thousands of miles from their feeding grounds to mate and lay eggs on the beach where they were born.

Wild But True!

The green sea turtle is named for its skin color—its shell, or carapace, is brown or olive in color. Scientists think they're green because of their seaweed and seagrass diet.

SUNNY SHORES

Though most green sea turtles stay underwater as much as possible, some will occasionally warm themselves by sunbathing on land.

HAIRY FROGFISH

SCIENTIFIC NAME
Antennarius striatus
LENGTH
4 to 10 inches
DIET Carnivore
LOCATION
Coastal temperate waters

The Latin *antenna* refers to the appendage on this fish's head.

Also known as a striated frogfish, this creature is covered in hairlike spines that enable it to blend perfectly into a background of coral. When an unsuspecting fish swims by, the hairy frogfish swallows it up before it has even realized a predator was there.

This unusual fish also has one particularly long spine which it likes to dangle in front of its mouth, tricking other fish into thinking it's a worm—the perfect snack. But if a fish is lured in by the bait, it becomes the snack!

TAKE A WALK

These abnormal fish can't swim. Instead, they use their wide fins to walk along the seafloor as they look for their next meal.

Wild But True!

The hairy frogfish can change color in order to blend in with its surroundings.

HUMBOLDT SQUID

SCIENTIFIC NAME
Dosidicus gigas

Gigas is Latin for "giant."

LENGTH
6 to 7 feet
DIET Carnivore
LOCATION
Eastern Pacific
Ocean, from South
America to Alaska

Squids have eight arms and two additional tentacles, which they use to bring their meals to their beak-like mouths. They move forward by propulsion, drawing water into the main parts of their bodies and then forcing it out, rocketing them where they want to go.

The Humboldt squid's arms are lined with sharp hooks on its suckers, which it uses to grab and pull apart its food. These squids have also been seen hunting cooperatively, something that scientists haven't observed in many other invertebrates.

COLOR CHANGER

Humboldt squids are able to change both the texture and color of their skin. When threatened they turn a bright red color, a trait that earned them the nickname "red devils."

Wild But True!

When a squid feels threatened, it can shoot out a cloud of dark ink, helping it escape from any nearby predators.

HUMPBACK WHALE

SCIENTIFIC NAME
Megaptera novaeangliae

LENGTH
48 to 62.5 feet

DIET Omnivore

LOCATION
Temperate waters

In Greek, mega means "large" and ptera means "wing."

Humpback whales are famous for their "songs," which can go on for hours. Made up of all sorts of groans, howls and cries, they can be heard from extremely far away. Only male humpbacks sing these songs, making scientists think they are a means of attracting a mate.

Humpbacks are also known for jumping out of the water, which is called breaching. They do this by propelling themselves upward with their extremely strong tail fins. It's unknown why humpbacks do this—it might be to help clean themselves or it might just be for fun!

SLOW AND STEADY

Humpback whales are fairly slow-moving creatures, mostly traveling at 9 miles per hour.

Wild But True!

Most humpbacks migrate to polar waters in order to feed, except for ones that live in the Arabian Sea.

MOBULA RAY

SCIENTIFIC NAME
Mobula mobular
LENGTH
Up to 17 feet
DIET Carnivore
LOCATION
Mediterranean Sea
coasts

Mobula may refer to the Latin *mobilis*, meaning "mobile."

NATURAL TALENT

Mobula rays are just as good at swimming as they are at acrobatics. Baby mobulas, or pups, immediately unfurl their fins and begin gliding through the water.

Mobula rays are closely related to sharks, but their behavior is pretty different. These fish travel in large groups and seem to constantly be putting on a show, jumping up to 6 feet out of the water and flipping and twirling as they splash back down. Scientists aren't sure whether this is just done for fun or if it's a form of communication, how they show off for potential mates or even a way to rid themselves of parasites.

NARWHAL

SCIENTIFIC NAME
Monodon monoceros
LENGTH 13 to 20 feet
DIET Carnivore
LOCATION Arctic coastal waters and rivers

In Greek, *mono* means "one" and *ceros* means "horn."

Known as the unicorn of the sea, narwhals have a single spiral tusk—really, a tooth—growing right through their upper lips. Though both male and female narwhals can have these tusks, the males' are much more prominent, growing up to almost 9 feet long.

Scientists aren't sure why narwhals have these impressive tusks. However, recent studies show the tooth is "inside out," with a softer outside and a harder inside, making scientists think it may be a sensory organ.

Wild But True!

Aside from the sizable tusk, narwhals don't have teeth in their mouths.

UNDERWATER CHITCHAT

Like other whales, narwhals communicate with a series of clicks, squeaks and whistles.

NILE CROCODILE

In Greek, *krokodeilos* means "pebble worm."

SCIENTIFIC NAME *Crocodylus niloticus*
LENGTH 16 feet
DIET Carnivore
LOCATION Rivers, marshes and swamps of sub-Saharan Africa, the Nile Basin and Madagascar

Nile crocodiles mostly eat fish, but that doesn't mean you should feel safe around them—these giant predators are likely to attack just about any animal in their line of sight, including zebras, porcupines, hippos and even other crocodiles.

They also have a very large appetite, eating up to half their body weight in one sitting. That's quite a lot—most Nile crocs weigh about 500 pounds, but they can weigh more than three times that.

PROUD PARENTS

While many reptiles don't watch over their eggs, both mother and father Nile crocodiles will guard over their nests until the eggs have hatched. They may even gently roll the eggs in their mouths to help their hatchlings emerge.

Wild But True!

When a crocodile closes its mouth, most of its lower teeth are visible—this is one of the ways you can tell a crocodile from an alligator.

ORCA

SCIENTIFIC NAME
Orcinus orca
LENGTH
23 to 32 feet
DIET Carnivore
LOCATION
Oceans

In Greek, *óryx* refers to "a kind of marine mammal."

O rcas are also called "killer whales," and it's easy to see why. Orcas have a set of 4-inch teeth that they put to very good use: They hunt marine mammals, fish, squid and seabirds, and have even been known to snatch seals right off the ice.

Orcas travel and hunt in large groups called pods. They're very intelligent sea creatures, often working together to create large waves that will sweep seals or penguins off the ice floes and into the water.

Wild But True!

Though they're called killer whales, orcas are actually the largest species of dolphin. The name is a reference to the fact that they're known for hunting whales.

TIGHT KNIT FAMILY

Orca calves will live with their mothers for at least two years, but many live with their families for their entire lives.

OYSTER

SCIENTIFIC NAME
Ostreidae
LENGTH
3 to 14 inches
DIET Carnivore
LOCATION
Temperate coastal
waters of North
America, South
America, Europe and
southern Australia

In Greek,
ostéon
means
"bone."

Oysters are a type of bivalve mollusk, meaning they have protective shells through which they filter water, letting them eat any algae or small food particle which passes through. Their shells protect their bodies, which are extremely vulnerable. When threatened, oysters use their extremely strong muscles to keep their shells closed.

Oysters are only mobile for the first few weeks of their lives. Once an oyster settles down, it attaches itself to an object, often another oyster's shell. By doing this, large colonies of oyster reefs are formed.

PEARL PRODUCERS

Though food oysters can produce pearls, pearl oysters are a distinct family from "true" oysters. Pearls are formed when sand or food slips between the oyster's shell and protective membrane, causing the oyster to protect itself by covering the irritant in layers of nacre, the same mineral its shell is made of.

Wild But True!

An oyster will switch between male and female at least once during its lifetime.

PIRANHA

SCIENTIFIC NAME
Pygocentrus
LENGTH
10 to 20 inches
DIET Carnivore
LOCATION
South American
freshwaters

In Greek, *kéntron* means "sharp point" or "thorn."

Piranhas have a reputation for being pretty fearsome fish—their name literally means "tooth fish" in Portuguese. However, while they do have very sharp teeth, they're generally not a threat to humans. In fact, one species of piranha is vegetarian, living entirely off riverweeds.

When piranhas do hunt, it's usually for fish smaller than they are. Piranhas often attack a prey's eyes and tail first, making it very difficult for an injured fish to escape.

BIG BARK

Red-bellied piranhas are known for their barking, a noise they make to warn other fish. If this escalates to a fight, the piranha will make grunting noises.

Wild But True!

Piranhas travel in packs, but because they are vulnerable to many larger creatures, this is thought to be for defense, not for hunting. Safety in numbers!

PUFFERFISH

SCIENTIFIC NAME
Tetraodontidae
LENGTH Up to 3 feet
DIET Omnivore
LOCATION Temperate oceans

In Latin, this name means "four teeth."

Pufferfish have some very interesting and unusual ways to defend themselves, which they likely developed because they are slow and clumsy swimmers. All pufferfish have elastic stomachs and the ability to draw in a large amount of water, enabling them to "puff" themselves up when threatened by a predator. They turn into a hard-to-eat ball more than twice their normal size!

Some pufferfish also have prickly spines on their bodies, making them even more unappetizing to predators. And finally, almost all pufferfish contain a toxin that makes them taste bad and is deadly to many fish.

SO MANY SPECIES

There are more than 120 kinds of pufferfish. Though they all have narrow bodies and round heads, there is a wide range in colors and sizes.

Wild But True!

In Japan, pufferfish is called fugu and specially trained chefs will serve it as a delicacy. It's a very risky meal, as consumers must trust the chefs to properly cut the fish to serve nontoxic meat.

SEA OTTER

SCIENTIFIC NAME
Enhydra lutris
LENGTH
4 feet
DIET Carnivore
LOCATION Pacific
Coasts of North
America and Asia

In Greek, *en* means ". in " and *hydra* means "water."

Wild But True!

A sea otter's fur is water-repellent, keeping the animal warm and dry while it swims.

Sea otters are mammals that spend much more time in the water than on land. They even sleep in the water, floating peacefully in large groups on their backs. Sometimes otters will sleep in large patches of kelp or seaweed so they don't float too far while they're resting.

These cute animals are also intelligent scavengers. Sea otters eat many small sea creatures but will also take their time opening clams and mussels by hitting them with rocks while they float on their backs.

WATER BABIES

Sea otters are the only otters to give birth to their young in water. Mothers will float on their backs to nurse the newborn pups and, soon after, teach them to swim.

177

SEAHORSE

SCIENTIFIC NAME
Hippocampus
LENGTH
0.6 to 14 inches
DIET Carnivore
LOCATION
Coastal waters

In Greek, *hippo* means "horse" and *kampos* means "sea monster."

Seahorses are one of the oddest-looking creatures in the sea. They move forward using just one small fin on their back, which can flutter up to 35 times per second. This is a very inefficient means of travel, and seahorses have been known to die of exhaustion when caught in rough waters.

Interestingly, seahorses don't have teeth or stomachs. Because they digest their food so quickly, they must eat almost constantly.

ANCHORS AWAY

Seahorses use their tails to anchor themselves to coral or sea grasses—once steady, they feed by sucking in any plankton or small crustaceans drifting by.

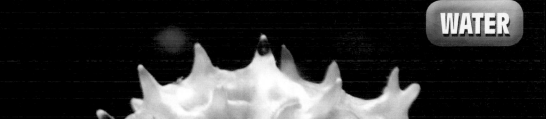

Wild But True!

Seahorses are the only known animal species in which the male carries their unborn young— they have a pouch on their front-facing side in which the female deposits her eggs.

STARFISH

SCIENTIFIC NAME
Asteroidea
LENGTH
4.7 to 9.4 inches
DIET Carnivore
LOCATION Oceans

In Greek, *asterias* means "starry."

A starfish's bony skin makes for a great defense from most predators—they're a pretty unappetizing meal. Their bright colors also scare off other creatures and serve as camouflage for hiding among reefs.

Starfish have the rare ability to digest prey outside their bodies. First they pry open clams or oysters using the suction cup-like tubes on their arms. Then their stomach oozes out from their mouth and into the freshly opened shell. The stomach surrounds its meal, digests it and is finally pulled back inside the starfish's body.

Wild But True!

Technically starfish aren't fish—they're classified as echinoderms. Because of this, scientists have begun calling them "sea stars."

A LOT OF ARMS

There are about 2,000 different species of starfish in the world. Many have five arms, but some have 10, 20 or even 40. As if that weren't enough, starfish also have the ability to regenerate their limbs if they lose one.

QUICK QUIZ

1 How do beluga whales navigate underwater?
- A. By sight
- B. By water temperature
- C. By echolocation

2 Which of the following animals is an invertebrate?
- A. Jellyfish
- B. Dolphin
- C. Sea Turtle

3 Where do green sea turtles lay their eggs?
- A. Underwater
- B. On a sandy shore
- C. In a cave

4 Do narwhals really have horns?
- A. Yes, they use them for fighting.
- B. No, their "horns" are actually a single tusk.
- C. Narwhals aren't real.

5 In which animal species does the male carry the young before they're born?
- A. Starfish
- B. Sea Otter
- C. Seahorse

6 What kind of animal is an orca?
- A. Dolphin
- B. Whale
- C. Fish

SEA CREATURE SNICKERS

Why do fish live in salt water?
Because pepper makes them sneeze!

How do oysters call their friends?
On shell phones!

Where do sea creatures go to hear music?
The orca-stra!

What do dolphins take to stay healthy?
Vitamin sea!

What is a shark's favorite sandwich?
Peanut butter and jellyfish!

What do whales like to chew?
Blubber gum!

FINDING OUT ABOUT
FORESTS

About 30 percent of Earth's land is covered in forests! Forests get up to 60 inches of rain per year and are filled with trees, shrubs and bushes.

FORESTS ARE FOUND ALL OVER THE WORLD. LIKE GRASSLANDS, THEY'RE ON EVERY CONTINENT EXCEPT ANTARCTICA.

Forest Layers

The topmost layer of a forest, where the upper parts of the tallest trees are, is called a canopy. The middle layer, called the understory, is made up of smaller trees and shrubs. The lowest layer is the forest floor, which has a variety of wildflowers, mosses, herbs and mushrooms.

WORLD

Temperate forests don't get as cold as the poles or as hot as deserts. They're generally between −20 degrees F and 90 degrees F. They experience four distinct seasons and have very fertile soil thanks to tree and plant leaves, which fall and decompose each autumn and winter.

WILD WORLD RECORDS

FOREST ANIMALS ARE USUALLY NOT THE BIGGEST OR FASTEST, BUT THEY HAVE PLENTY OF OTHER AMAZING ATTRIBUTES.

BEST ARCHITECT ON LAND
BEAVER

At 2,790 feet, the world's largest beaver dam is twice the length of the Hoover Dam.

MOST ADAPTABLE
RAT

No other creature has dominated the world quite like the humble rat, a species that has thrived almost everywhere on Earth (except Antarctica).

BEST THIEF
RACCOON

Not only do they naturally have face masks, raccoons are famously able to open locks and jars.

PRICKLIEST PROTECTION
PORCUPINE
With more than 30,000 quills, these rodents are rarely bothered by the same animal more than once.

FANCIEST FEATHERS
INDIAN PEAFOWL
There are plenty of eye-catching birds, but a peacock's iridescent tail feathers steal the show.

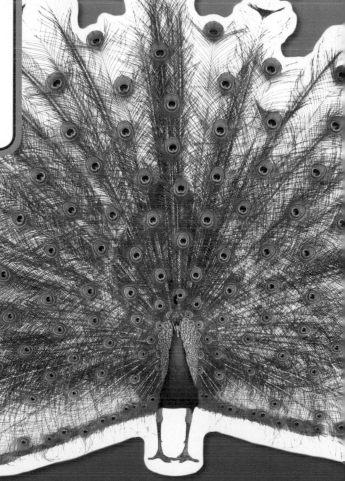

FIVE FACTS ABOUT THE REDWOOD FORESTS

THE REDWOOD TREES IN CALIFORNIA'S REDWOOD FORESTS ARE THE TALLEST LIVING THINGS ON EARTH.

1 The biggest tree in the redwood forests is 379 feet tall and named Hyperion.

2 Most trees in the forest are around 2,000 years old and more than 250 feet tall.

3 The trees have survived for so long thanks to their incredibly thick bark, which withstands forest fires and wood-eating termites.

4 More than 200 different species of vertebrates (animals with spines) live in redwood forests, including snakes, lizards, frogs, toads, birds, bats, squirrels, weasels, bears, elk and deer.

5 The Redwood National Parks have more than 200 miles of trails for hikers to wander along.

AMERICAN MARTEN

SCIENTIFIC NAME
Martes americana
LENGTH
18.5 to 27 inches
DIET Omnivore
LOCATION
North America

Martes is Latin for "warlike spirit."

Don't be fooled by these furry little creatures' adorable looks—they're expert hunters! American martens particularly like to prey on red squirrels, occasionally chasing them through trees. If it catches one, the marten will quickly kill the squirrel with a bite to the back of its neck.

American martens are very reserved creatures, but sometimes their curiosity gets the best of them. If you live near them, you might even see one peeking in your window.

BIG FEET

American martens have comparatively big feet for their body size. This is helpful when they need to walk through snow—it's like they have their own snowshoes.

Wild But True!

American martens have semi-retractable claws, similar to a cat's.

ASIATIC BLACK BEAR

SCIENTIFIC NAME *Ursus thibetanus*
LENGTH 4 to 6.25 feet
DIET Omnivore
LOCATION Central, Eastern and Southern Asia

Thibetanus means "Tibetan."

Like other bears, Asiatic black bears will eat meat but mostly fill up on plants instead. They have very long snouts and an excellent sense of smell, which they depend on to help them find their next meal—especially because their senses of sight and hearing aren't very good.

Asiatic black bears do have one big difference from other species of bear: they're nocturnal. They spend their days asleep in tree hollows, nests or caves, and emerge at night to search for food.

UP IN THE TREES

Asiatic black bears spend about half their time in trees and even build platforms so they can relax and feed. They're like treehouses for bears!

Wild But True!
These bears are sometimes called "moon bears" because of the crescent-shaped pale markings on their chests.

BARRED OWL

SCIENTIFIC NAME
Strix varia
LENGTH 21 inches
WINGSPAN
43 inches
DIET Carnivore
LOCATION Eastern
North America,
Central Canada,
California

Varia comes from the Latin word varius, meaning "diverse."

OUT AND ABOUT

The barred owl is generally nocturnal, but they can occasionally be seen (or heard) hunting and hooting during the day.

Barred owls are very territorial birds which live their entire lives in the same area—they're not migrators. They mostly eat small mammals but will hunt just about anything, including lizards, other birds, insects, frogs and even fish.

These owls are very vocal birds, known for their loud hoots. When the barred owl finds a mate, the two will hoot together—you can pick out the male's voice as deeper and more mellow.

Wild But True!

Many people who hear the barred owl's call think it sounds like someone is shouting the phrase, "Who cooks for you-all?"

BROWN RAT

SCIENTIFIC NAME
Rattus norvegicus
LENGTH
16 to 20 inches
DIET Omnivore
LOCATION
Everywhere but the
poles and deserts

This means
"Norway rat,"
though they had
not made it there
when they got
this name.

Scientists think the brown rat originated in Asia, but this highly adaptable mammal found its way onto trade ships and now can live anywhere in the world it can find food and shelter. This is because they'll eat just about anything and are prolific breeders, birthing up to 60 young per year.

Brown rats prefer to live in underground burrows, where they've built spaces for nesting and food storage. Well-traveled passageways within the burrows are scent-marked with urine.

BLIND AS A RAT
Brown rats have poor vision, but they make up for this with their strong senses of smell and hearing.

Wild But True!

Rats are extremely agile in water, able to swim distances of up to 2,000 feet.

BURMESE PYTHON

SCIENTIFIC NAME *Python bivitattus*
LENGTH 16 to 23 feet
DIET Carnivore
LOCATION Southeast Asia, Florida Everglades

Bivittatus means "doub striped" in Latin.

Burmese pythons can't see very well, but they make up for this in a pretty fascinating way, using chemical receptors in their tongues and heat-sensors in their jaws in order to find their prey. Once a python finds its next meal, it wraps its body around the animal and squeezes, suffocating it. Then, making good use of the stretchy ligaments in its mouth, the Burmese python swallows its prey whole.

ESCAPE ARTISTS

Burmese pythons are an "invasive species" in Florida. Many of the snakes escaped zoos and pet shops after destruction from Hurricane Andrew in 1992, and now it's believed that tens of thousands of them dwell in the Everglades.

Wild But True!

Burmese pythons are very good swimmers and can stay underwater for up to 30 minutes before resurfacing for air.

201

CANADA GOOSE

SCIENTIFIC NAME
Branta canadensis
LENGTH
30 to 43 inches
WINGSPAN
4.2 to 5.6 feet
DIET Herbivore
LOCATION
United States
and Canada

Branta comes from the Old Norse brandgás, meaning "burnt goose."

C anada geese are famous for flying together in a "V" shape, something they do during their yearly migrations. The journey from Canada to the southern United States is a long one, and the birds have specific "rest stops" they make along the same path each year.

However, not all Canada geese migrate. Many have decided to make permanent homes in the warmer climates of North America, much to the chagrin of airports, parks and golf courses all over the United States.

Wild But True!

When flying with the wind, these geese can travel up to 1,500 miles in just 24 hours.

HONK, HONK

Canada geese make a distinctive honking noise. They use it to communicate with one another while migrating and to warn other animals off their territory during mating season.

COATI

SCIENTIFIC NAME
Nasua nasua

LENGTH
13 to 24 inches

DIET Omnivore

LOCATION North America, South America

In Latin, *nasus* means "nose."

The cuddly coati is closely related to raccoons and even shares their trademark ringed tail. Unlike raccoons, the coati is a diurnal creature. While racoons prefer to venture out at night, the coati spends the evenings slumbering in trees—their babies, or kittens, sleep in nests made out of twigs and leaves.

The coati spends most of its day searching for food, using its long snout to search in crevices and holes for fruits, insects, rodents and small reptiles to snack on.

TAILS UP

The coati has a semi-prehensile tail that is almost as long as its body. It uses the tail for balance, but it is not strong enough to be used as an extra limb, like a monkey's tail.

Wild But True!

A coati likes to sleep curled up with its nose tucked into its stomach.

205

DOWNY WOODPECKER

SCIENTIFIC NAME
Dryobates pubescens
LENGTH 6 inches
WINGSPAN
10 to 12 inches
DIET Omnivore
LOCATION
North America

In Ancient Greek, *dryobates* means "woodland walker."

These woodpeckers are the smallest in North America, but they don't mind. Their small size lets them eat insects that larger birds can't get to, like those living in the stems of weeds.

Downy woodpeckers prefer to nest in dead trees or the dead part of a living tree. This makes building the nest easier, since dead wood is often softer and easier for them to carve into. A male and female will work together to build their nest, a process that takes up to three weeks.

STAND OFF

When downy woodpeckers get into tiffs with one another, they make a show of swinging their beaks from side to side and spreading out their head and tail feathers.

Wild But True!

Woodpeckers don't sing songs, but they do make music by pecking on wood and metal.

EASTERN CHIPMUNK

SCIENTIFIC NAME *Tamias striatus*
LENGTH 7 to 11 inches
DIET Omnivore
LOCATION Eastern
United States and Canada

In Greek, *tamias* means "treasurer" or "storer."

Like many other small mammals, eastern chipmunks are excellent burrowers. They dig intricate underground systems in which to live and spend all of winter underground. Chipmunks are very protective of their burrows and will defend them to the best of their ability, chasing and fighting with any chipmunk that tries to invade their space.

Chipmunks are also very vocal, making a lot of loud "chips" and "cuk-cuk-cuk" noises in order to let others know predators are nearby, or to announce to rival chipmunks that they are encroaching on their territory.

TEMPORARY TORPOR

Chipmunks don't exactly hibernate, but they enter a similar state known as a "torpor." When it's very cold out, they'll go into this mode of inactivity for a few days as a way to conserve energy.

Wild But True!

Chipmunks like to "scatter hoard," or deposit small amounts of food in various areas, in case their main food stores are stolen or destroyed. It's always good to have a backup snack!

EASTERN COTTONTAIL RABBIT

SCIENTIFIC NAME *Sylvilagus floridanus*
LENGTH 15.5 to 18.75 inches
DIET Herbivore
LOCATION Eastern North America to South America

Silva means "forest" in Latin, while lagos means "hare" in Greek.

Eastern cottontail rabbits are big grass eaters, though they'll happily munch on vegetables in a garden if they're lucky enough to find one. In the winter, these mammals need to make do with whatever twigs and bark they can find.

Eastern cottontails also look a bit different in winter than they do in summer. During cold weather, their coat grows out, becoming long and gray. When the weather warms up again, they'll shed this coat, revealing shorter brown fur.

Wild But True!

Eastern cottontails will run from predators in one of two ways: by running in a zigzag pattern or slinking away close to the ground with their ears lowered.

EARLY LEARNERS

Eastern cottontail rabbits are born blind and without fur, but they mature very quickly and can take care of themselves just weeks after being born.

GARTER SNAKE

In Greek, *thamnos* means "shrub."

SCIENTIFIC NAME
Thamnophis sirtalis
LENGTH 23 to 30 inches
DIET Carnivore
LOCATION North America

These non-venomous snakes are extremely common and mostly harmless. When threatened, a garter snake may attempt to strike, but more likely will release a foul-smelling secretion from its anal gland. Garter snakes will also coil themselves when threatened, making them appear slightly larger than they really are.

Garter snakes are mostly solitary but group together when the weather gets colder, sleeping or hibernating together in tight coils so they can maintain a safe body temperature.

Wild But True!

Garter snakes communicate via pheromones. They pick up the scents with their tongues, then insert their tongue into a special organ in their mouth that can interpret the signal.

SUPER SMELL

These snakes have an excellent sense of smell, which they use to find their prey and other snakes.

GRAY WOLF

SCIENTIFIC NAME
Canis lupus
LENGTH 4.5 to 6 feet
DIET Carnivore
LOCATION Alaska, Canada, Asia

In Latin, *canis* means "dog" and *lupus* means "wolf."

Wolves are the largest members of the dog family, usually weighing around 135 pounds—though some wolves can weigh up to a whopping 175 pounds! They live in packs of about six, though packs of more than 30 wolves have been observed.

Because they live and hunt together, communication is very important to wolves. They use body language, scents produced by their bodies and various howls, barks, whimpers, yips and snarls to convey messages to one another.

Wild But True!

A wolf's sense of smell is 100 times stronger than a human's.

HANDY HOWLS

A wolf's howl can be heard from up to 10 miles away! A single wolf howls to get the attention of its pack, while groups of wolves howling usually means they are sending territorial messages.

HEDGEHOG

SCIENTIFIC NAME
Erinaceus europaeus
LENGTH
5 to 14 inches
DIET Carnivore
LOCATION Africa,
Europe and Asia

Erinaceus means "hedgehog" in Latin.

Though they're not related to pigs, hedgehogs make grunting sounds just like them. They're particularly noisy when rooting through hedges looking for a small animal to snack on, hence their name.

Hedgehogs are immune to some poisonous plants. Sometimes, for extra protection, they will eat one of these plants just so they can lick their coat afterward. Scientists think this either masks the hedgehog's scent or punishes any predator that tries to eat it!

Wild But True!

Hedgehogs don't have very good eyesight and hunt for their food mostly through hearing and smell.

PRICKLY PROTECTION

When threatened, a hedgehog will curl up, effectively turning itself into a ball covered in pointy spines—not an appetizing meal for predators. Hedgehogs also sleep in this position during the day.

217

INDIAN PEAFOWL

SCIENTIFIC NAME
Pavo cristatus
LENGTH
8 to 9 feet
WINGSPAN
4.5 to 5.25 feet
DIET Omnivore
LOCATION
Southern Asia

In Latin, *cristatus* means "crested."

Weighing up to 13 pounds, peafowl are one of the largest kinds of birds that are still able to fly. The males, called peacocks, have colorful tails that make them vulnerable to predators, but luckily, the tail feathers come out very easily, enabling peacocks to fly away if another animal manages to latch on.

Peahens, the females, are not nearly as flashy looking as their male counterparts. Scientists think this is so they can better blend in with surroundings, an important feature for when they protect their eggs.

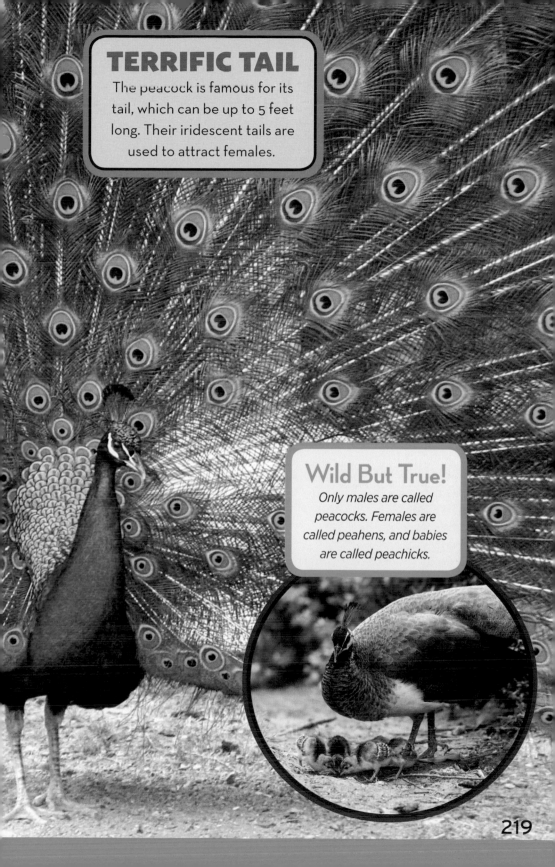

TERRIFIC TAIL

The peacock is famous for its tail, which can be up to 5 feet long. Their iridescent tails are used to attract females.

Wild But True!

Only males are called peacocks. Females are called peahens, and babies are called peachicks.

JAGUAR

SCIENTIFIC NAME *Panthera onca*
LENGTH 4 to 6 feet
DIET Carnivore
LOCATION
Northern South America

Onça is Portuguese for jaguar.

The jaguar is the third-largest wild cat in the world—only lions and tigers are bigger. As such, jaguars are rightly at the top of the food chain in South America.

Though their adult lives are spent mostly alone, jaguars spend their first two years with their mothers, who protect them and teach them how to hunt. These sly cats will lie in wait in a tree branch, then ambush their prey by leaping down and killing with one strong bite.

STRONG SWIMMER

Unlike many other cats, jaguars love the water and do much of their hunting there, preying on fish, turtles and caimans (a smaller relative of alligators).

Wild But True!

The name jaguar comes from the Native American word yaguar, meaning "he who kills with one leap."

KING COBRA

SCIENTIFIC NAME
Ophiophagus hannah
LENGTH Up to 18 feet
DIET Carnivore
LOCATION India, Southern China, Southeast Asia

Ophiophagus comes from the Greek words for "snake-eating."

King cobras can eat warm-blooded mammals, and often do in captivity. But in the wild, these snakes prefer to dine on cold-blooded creatures, especially other snakes.

Though king cobras usually don't attack when threatened (they prefer to slither away), they are very intimidating when they do prepare to strike. Lifting the front of its head up to 6 feet off the ground, the king cobra will follow its attacker for long distances, all while hissing and flattening its neck ribs into a hood. A female cobra protecting her eggs is much more likely to fight back than most other cobras.

NATURE'S NESTER

King cobras are the only snakes that build nests for their eggs.

Wild But True!

A king cobra's fangs angle back into the reptile's mouth, helping push prey down its throat and toward the stomach.

MALLARD DUCK

SCIENTIFIC NAME *Anas platyrhynchos*
LENGTH 20 to 35 inches
WINGSPAN 3 feet   **DIET** Omnivore
LOCATION North America, Europe, Asia and Southern Australia

In Greek, *platurrhunkhos* means "broad-snouted."

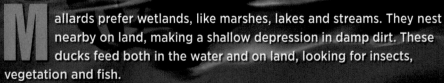

Mallards prefer wetlands, like marshes, lakes and streams. They nest nearby on land, making a shallow depression in damp dirt. These ducks feed both in the water and on land, looking for insects, vegetation and fish.

There are a few big differences between male and female mallard ducks. Only the males have green heads—the females are mostly gray and brown. Females are also the only ones that quack, while males make deeper, short calls.

Wild But True!

A mallard duck's outer layer of feathers is waterproof. It's covered in an oil that is secreted from a gland near its tail.

DABBLE DINNER

Mallard ducks don't dive for their food—instead, they "dabble" for it by leaning forward, leaving their rears and tails pointed up and out of the water. Sometimes they will balance themselves by wagging their feet or waving their tails in this position.

MOUNTAIN GOAT

In Greek, *oros* means "mountain" and *amnos* means "lamb."

SCIENTIFIC NAME *Oreamnos americanus*
LENGTH 5.5 feet
DIET Herbivore
LOCATION Northwestern North America

Native to the Rocky and Cascade mountains, these mammals are incredible climbers. A mountain goat's hooves are very wide, which is good for balance, and have rough pads on the bottom, giving them excellent traction. They're also extremely agile, able to jump almost 12 feet.

Male mountain goats are called "billies" and females are called "nannies." After a female mountain goat gives birth to a kid, the newborn will be able to climb around by the next day.

Wild But True!

Mountain goats are actually goat-antelopes. They are more closely related to antelopes, gazelles and cattle than actual goats.

HIDDEN IN THE SNOW

A mountain goat's white coat helps it camouflage into its snowy habitat.

NORTH AMERICAN BEAVER

SCIENTIFIC NAME
Castor canadensis
LENGTH
2 to 3 feet
DIET Herbivore
LOCATION
North America

In Greek, *Kastor* means "he who excels."

Weighing up to 60 pounds, beavers are the largest rodents in North America. They move somewhat uncomfortably on land, but are better suited to the water, swimming up to 5 miles per hour with their webbed feet and able to stay submerged for up to 15 minutes. Beavers are famous for building dams, which create a new habitat for them and lots of other creatures: ponds with slow-moving water. The dams are built from sticks, branches and saplings which the beavers then caulk with mud to make watertight.

Wild But True!

A beaver has very sensitive whiskers that it uses to help detect nearby objects while navigating narrow passages and swimming in dark waters.

HELPFUL TAIL

A beaver's tail serves as a rudder while swimming, as a way to balance on land and even as a signal for danger when slapped on water. Beavers can also live off the fat in their tails if food is scarce.

NORTH AMERICAN PORCUPINE

SCIENTIFIC NAME
Erethizon dorsatum
LENGTH
2 to 3 feet
DIET Herbivore
LOCATION
North America

Loosely translated, this means "the animal with the irritating back."

The porcupine is the prickliest species of rodent. Each can have more than 30,000 quills, which they use to protect themselves. If another animal attacks the porcupine, the quills can detach and lodge in the predator, causing painful wounds.

North American porcupines are the largest species of porcupine, and they're surprisingly good climbers—you might spot one in a tree! They use their large front teeth to munch on the tree's bark and stems.

ADAPTABLE ANIMAL

Though North American porcupines live in the forest, other species in Asia, Europe and Africa have adapted to deserts and grasslands.

Wild But True!

When a baby porcupine is born, its quills are soft! They'll harden within a few days.

NORTH AMERICAN RACCOON

SCIENTIFIC NAME *Procyon lotor*
LENGTH 24 to 38 inches
DIET Omnivore
LOCATION North America

In Latin, *lotor* means "washer."

Raccoons live all over North America, mostly because they aren't picky about what they eat, from fruits and vegetables to mice, insects and bird or reptile eggs. They even use their small hands to snatch swimming crayfish and frogs right from the water, a habit that likely contributes to the myth that these creatures wash their food before eating it.

Being open to eating nearly anything enables raccoons in colder climates to store a lot before winter. When the cold weather comes, they'll spend most of the season asleep in their dens.

UP IN THE TREES

Raccoons prefer to make their homes in hollow trees, though they will take shelter just about anywhere they can find it.

Wild But True!

A raccoon is very intelligent and has incredible dexterity, a combination that enables it to open latches, doors, jars and bottles.

SQUIRREL

SCIENTIFIC NAME
Sciuridae
LENGTH
5 to 36 inches
DIET Omnivore
LOCATION
Everywhere
except Australia
and the Poles

In Greek, *skiouros* means "shadow-tailed."

Though Americans are mostly familiar with tree squirrels, there are more than 200 species of squirrels around the world, including the Indian giant squirrel, which can be up to 3 feet long. There are three main kinds of squirrels: ground squirrels, tree squirrels and flying squirrels.

Most kinds of squirrels like to bury their food underground so it can be recovered later. They're capable of locating food buried under a foot of snow, but squirrels usually bury much more food than they'll need to get through the winter. Any forgotten acorns will eventually grow into trees!

TREMENDOUS TEETH

Like other rodents, squirrels have front teeth that never stop growing. This may sound annoying, but it's perfect for animals that are always gnawing on something and filing down their chompers.

Wild But True!

A group of squirrels is referred to as a scurry.

VAMPIRE BAT

Vampire bats, which have shorter torsos than most other bats, got their name for a somewhat chilling reason: they're the only mammals that live entirely off blood (except for their young, which survive off their mother's milk). These bats usually feed from sleeping horses or cattle, a process that takes about half an hour. Unlike fictional vampires, they don't suck the blood: after biting their victim, the bat laps up the blood with its tongue. The vampire bat's saliva keeps the blood from clotting.

STRANGE SLEEPERS

Vampire bats sleep upside down, hanging from the roof of a cave. They usually live in groups of about 100, but colonies of more than 1,000 have been reported.

Wild But True!

Vampire bats have heat sensors on their noses, helping them find the perfect place to feed on an animal.

VIRGINIA OPOSSUM

SCIENTIFIC NAME
Didelphis virginiana
LENGTH 2.5 feet
DIET Omnivore
LOCATION North America

In Latin, *di* means "two" and *delphús* means "womb."

The Virginia opossum has the distinction of being the only marsupial, or pouched mammal, living in the United States. After being born, baby opossums, called joeys, are as small as honeybees. They immediately climb into their mother's pouch to finish developing. In this sense, it's almost like they have two wombs.

Once a joey is a little older, it will begin leaving its mother's pouch, sometimes riding on her back while she scavenges for food.

PLAYING POSSUM

These creatures are famous for playing dead when a predator is near, flopping over, sticking out their tongues and closing their eyes or staring off blankly. Weirdly, it works: Since the predator isn't worried about its meal going anywhere, the opossum may get another opportunity to escape if the predator is distracted.

Wild But True!

Opossums are excellent at climbing trees and spend much of their time high off the ground.

WHITE-TAILED DEER

SCIENTIFIC NAME
Odocoileus virginianus
LENGTH
6 to 7.75 feet
DIET Herbivore
LOCATION
North America,
South America

In Latin, *odocoileus* means "hollow tooth."

White-tailed deer are mostly nocturnal creatures that like to do most of their grazing during dawn and dusk. They eat all kinds of plant life, including leaves, twigs, nuts, fruits, vegetables and even fungi. There is a hollow portion in the middle of their teeth.

Only male deer, or bucks, grow antlers. They use them to fight over females during the mating season. However, during the winter, you'd be hard-pressed to tell a buck from a doe, as the antlers fall off each year and are regrown in the spring.

Wild But True!

This deer's coat changes color, going from a reddish-brown in the summer to a grayish-brown in the winter.

INCREDIBLE LEAPER

Not only can these deer run up to 30 miles per hour, they can leap up to 10 feet high and 30 feet forward in one jump.

WOLVERINE

SCIENTIFIC NAME *Gulo gulo*
LENGTH 33 to 44 inches
DIET Omnivore
LOCATION Northern North America, Europe and Asia

In Latin, *gulo* means "glutton."

Wolverines do eat some vegetation, but they would much rather enjoy meat whenever possible. These mammals will roam up to 15 miles each day in search of prey, often rabbits and other rodents. However, they have been known to take down much larger animals, like caribou, if they're already injured. These ravenous critters will also eat any carcasses they can find, using their specialized molars to tear into frozen animals. In fact, their strong, sharp teeth even allow them to chew through bones.

Wild But True!

In the winter, wolverines will sometimes dig into burrows and eat hibernating animals.

SPECIAL PAWS

A wolverine's paws will spread out to twice their size when pressed to the ground, distributing its weight and letting it move quickly and easily over snow-covered grounds.

QUICK QUIZ

ARE YOU A FOREST EXPERT?

1 Can brown rats swim?
- A. No, they sink.
- B. Only for very short distances.
- C. Yes, very well.

2 In what shape do Canada geese fly when migrating?
- A. S
- B. F
- C. V

3 How do eastern cottontail rabbits evade predators?
- A. They run away in a zigzag pattern.
- B. They run in circles.
- C. They run away in a straight line.

4 How do hedgehogs get their name?
- A. They are very territorial of hedges.
- B. They grunt while looking for food in hedges.
- C. They look like hogs made out of hedges.

5 What kinds of peafowl have the flashiest feathers?
- A. Peacocks
- B. Peahens
- C. Peachicks

6 What part of a squirrel never stops growing?
- A. Its tail
- B. Its front teeth
- C. Its ears

FOREST FUNNIES

What is a garter snake's favorite subject?
Hisss-tory!

What is a bat's favorite thing to do?
Just hang out!

Why do geese fly south for the winter?
It's too far to walk!

What do you get when you cross a porcupine with a balloon?
POP!

How does a hedgehog play leapfrog?
Very carefully!

Why don't wolves make good dancers?
Because they have two left feet!

READY FOR
RAINFORESTS

About 6 percent of Earth's surface is covered in rainforests!
They get at least 98 inches of rain per year,
but sometimes as much as 177 inches.

AROUND THE

RAINFORESTS ARE FOUND IN AFRICA, SOUTHEAST ASIA, AUSTRALIA AND SOUTH AMERICA. LIKE FORESTS, RAINFORESTS ARE DIVIDED INTO THREE LAYERS: THE CANOPY, THE UNDERSTORY AND THE FOREST FLOOR.

WORLD

Unbelievable Biome

Even though rainforests are relatively small, scientists think about half of the planet's known plant and animal species can be found within them! The incredible density of trees and plants also make rainforests the "lungs" of the Earth: they produce about 40 percent of the world's oxygen and 20 percent of the world's freshwater.

WILD WORLD RECORDS

BECAUSE THEY CONTAIN HALF THE WORLD'S SPECIES, IT'S NO SURPRISE RAINFORESTS HAVE SOME PRETTY SPECTACULAR CREATURES!

STINKIEST SCUFFLER
RING-TAILED LEMUR
When male lemurs fight, they secrete a smelly substance and wave it around.

HEAVIEST (AND MOST COLORFUL) MONKEY
MANDRILL
Mandrills can weigh up to 110 pounds and boast bright blue, red and yellow faces.

LARGEST RODENT
CAPYBARA

Stretching up to 4.2 feet long with a maximum weight of 174 pounds, you better hope you never have a capybara infestation!

LAZIEST LOUNGER
THREE-TOED SLOTH

Not only do they move just 6 to 8 feet per minute, some male sloths spend their entire lives in the same tree.

HEAVIEST SNAKE
GREEN ANACONDA

Though they're not the longest, green anacondas can weigh up to 1,100 pounds!

FIVE FACTS ABOUT THE AMAZON BASIN

LOCATED IN SOUTH AMERICA, THE AMAZON BASIN IS WHAT MOST PEOPLE THINK OF WHEN TALKING ABOUT "THE RAINFOREST."

1 The Amazon Basin is the largest rainforest. It's about the size of the United States, with more than half of it located in Brazil.

2 It contains a multitude of different species, including 2.5 million different insects, 40,000 types of plants, 3,000 kinds of fish, 1,300 varieties of birds and 430 species of mammals.

3 The canopy layer is so thick it can take up to 10 minutes for a drop of water to reach the rainforest floor.

4 The Amazon has been around for about 55 million years!

5 At almost 4,000 miles long, the Amazon River is the second-longest in the world.

AMAZON TREE BOA

SCIENTIFIC NAME
Corallus hortulanus
LENGTH
4 to 7 feet
DIET Carnivore
LOCATION
Central and
South America

In Latin,
hortulanus
means
"gardener."

Sometimes referred to as a garden tree boa, this snake is often incredibly colorful, helping it blend in with its rainforest environment. Amazon tree boas can be brown or grey, but scientists have also documented red, orange and yellow variations.

Like many other boas, these nocturnal snakes have excellent heat sensors, which they use to find prey in the dead of night. They eat small mammals, reptiles and even birds!

A TAIL FOR TREES

Unsurprisingly, this tree boa spends most of its time aloft in trees. It uses its strong, prehensile tail to move more easily among the branches.

Wild But True!

In addition to heat sensors, Amazon tree boas have very good eyesight and may also hunt during the day.

BINTURONG

Sometimes called a bearcat because of its appearance, the binturong likes to spend its time high up in the trees. Up there is where all its favorite snacks are, including fruits, shoots, eggs and insects.

Because of its short limbs, the binturong isn't very good at climbing from tree to tree. Instead, it returns to the ground before ascending another one. It does have a neat trick when doing this, though: the binturong's ankles can turn 180 degrees, allowing them to easily climb head first down tree trunks.

Wild But True!
Binturongs produce a scent that smells like buttered popcorn! They use it to mark their territory and attract mates.

HANDY TAIL
The binturong has a prehensile tail that it uses like an extra limb when navigating trees in the rainforest.

BLUE POISON DART FROG

SCIENTIFIC NAME
Dendrobates tinctorius
LENGTH 1 inch
DIET Carnivore
LOCATION Northern South America

In Greek, *dendrobates* means "tree climber."

The incredibly tiny blue poison dart frog weighs less than 1 ounce but has an impressive defense mechanism: its poison skin, which can paralyze or even kill its predators. While this means adult blue poison dart frogs have very few threats, they are extremely vulnerable while they are still tadpoles.

Once grown, these frogs are diurnal creatures that spend much of the day foraging for food, usually any insects they find on the rainforest floor.

LAND LOVER

Unlike many other frogs, blue poison dart frogs lack webbing between their toes. This makes them poor swimmers, so they rarely go in water.

Wild But True!
This frog's bright color warns other predators not to eat it.

CAPYBARA

SCIENTIFIC NAME
Hydrochoerus
hydrochaeris
LENGTH
3 to 4.2 feet
DIET Herbivore
LOCATION Central
and South America

In Greek, *hydro* means "water" and *choiros* means "pig."

Weighing anywhere from 60 to 174 pounds, capybaras are the world's largest rodents. Like other rodents, they have front teeth that never stop growing. To file these teeth down and get all the nutrients they need, capybaras will spend most of the day chewing on grass and water plants. Because it's difficult to digest a lot of these plants, capys will sometimes regurgitate their food and chew it again, and also eat their own feces—the bacteria helps their stomachs digest more fiber.

Wild But True!
Like hippos and alligators, a capybara's eyes and nose are located near the top of its head, enabling it to stay mostly underwater while surveying its surroundings.

MADE FOR WATER
Capybaras feel right at home near a source of water like a riverbank or marsh. They love to eat the nearby plants and escape to the water when threatened.

CHIMPANZEE

SCIENTIFIC NAME
Pan troglodytes
LENGTH 4 to 5.5 feet
DIET Omnivore
LOCATION Central Africa

In Greek, troglodytes means "cave-dwelling."

Chimps like to spend their days up in the trees, easily swinging from branch to branch. They eat most of their meals up there and also sleep in nests made in the treetops. When on the ground, they usually move around on all fours, but can walk upright for short distances.

These mammals live in large groups and are very social, grooming one another and communicating with a wide range of facial expressions, gestures and noises.

TOOLING AROUND

Chimps are one of the few species that make and use tools. They often shape sticks to be used for digging grubs out of logs or use leaves to sponge up drinking water.

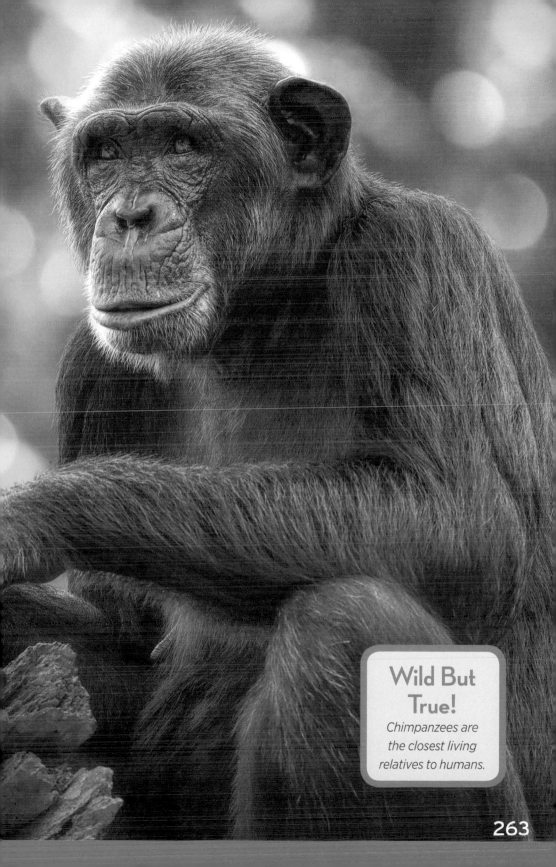

Wild But True!

Chimpanzees are the closest living relatives to humans.

CRAB-EATING MACAQUE

SCIENTIFIC NAME
Macaca fascicularis
LENGTH 15 to 22 inches
DIET Omnivore
LOCATION Southeast Asia

In Latin, *fascicularis* means a "small band or stripe."

Despite its name, the crab-eating macaque is largely a frugivore, meaning it mostly eats fruit. This primate is highly adaptable, however, and will eat just about anything it can find, including insects, reptiles, fish and amphibians. The crab-eating macaque is also an excellent swimmer. Its name likely comes from the fact that it likes to insert its hands in underwater burrows in the hopes of finding crabs or other shellfish. If it's lucky and finds a crab, the macaque will use a rock to break it open.

EXTENSIVE TAIL

The crab-eating macaque's long tail makes it easy to distinguish from other macaques. The tail is mostly used for balance when the macaque is moving among the trees.

Wild But True!

Like other macaques, these primates store food in their cheeks while foraging so they can eat it later.

GIANT PANDA

SCIENTIFIC NAME
Ailuropoda melanoleuca
LENGTH
4 to 6 feet
DIET Omnivore
LOCATION
Central China

In Greek, *Ailuropoda* means "cat-foot."

Though pandas can and do sometimes eat fish and small mammals, their diet is 99 percent bamboo. Bamboo isn't very nutritious, so pandas need to eat a lot of it—they spend up to 12 hours a day snacking on the fibrous plant.

A giant panda's teeth are perfect for munching on bamboo shoots, leaves and stems. Their wide and flat molars easily crush the bamboo, allowing the panda to quickly eat 1.5-inch stalks. They hold the stalks with extra-big wrist bones, which they use like thumbs.

COLOR-BLOCKED CAMOUFLAGE

Though it looks striking to us, the panda's black-and-white fur provides perfect camouflage in bamboo patches on snowy mountains.

GIANT ANTEATER

SCIENTIFIC NAME
Myrmecophaga tridactyla

In Latin, tridactyla means "three fingers."

LENGTH
40 to 48 inches
DIET Carnivore
LOCATION Central and South America

The giant anteater's tail can be almost 3 feet long, giving this mammal a total length of up to 7 feet! It feeds by using its claws to rip into an anthill and then, using its long tongue, the giant eater slurps up an incredible 35,000 ants per day.

Giant anteaters are also excellent swimmers, using their long legs to paddle and sticking their snouts high out of the water, using their noses like a snorkel!

CLEVER CLAWS

A giant anteater's claws are up to 4 inches long, helping it defend itself against jaguars.

Wild But True!

Anteaters are edentates—
they have no teeth! But
their long tongues can
reach up to 2 feet out
of their mouths.

GREEN ANACONDA

SCIENTIFIC NAME
Eunectes murinus
LENGTH Up to 36 feet
DIET Carnivore
LOCATION Northern South America

In Greek, *eunectes* means "good swimmer."

Weighing up to 1,100 pounds, green anacondas are the biggest of the anacondas, and the heaviest snakes in the world (the reticulated python can be slightly longer).

Though they're not venomous, anacondas are incredibly deadly. As part of the constrictor family, these snakes kill their prey by slowly squeezing it to death and then swallowing it whole, no matter how large an animal. If the meal was especially large, the anaconda can go months without feeding again.

PATIENT PREDATOR

A green anaconda likes to stay mostly hidden, and then suddenly ambush their unsuspecting meal.

Wild But True!

Green anacondas give birth to up to 36 live young at a time.

271

GREEN BASILISK LIZARD

SCIENTIFIC NAME
Basiliscus plumifrons
LENGTH 2 to 2.5 feet
DIET Omnivore
LOCATION Central America

Basilískos is Greek for "little king."

The green basilisk lizard lives in the rainforests of Central America, and always makes sure to stay close to a body of water. If a predator approaches, this lizard will make for the water and then run right across it, a trick it pulls off thanks to its extreme speed and long toes. By slapping their feet against the water, they create an air pocket that keeps them from dropping beneath the water's surface.

Wild But True!
Green basilisks can only run on water for about 15 feet, then they start to swim!

SUPER SWIMMER
Green basilisk lizards can stay underwater for up to half an hour.

LEOPARD

SCIENTIFIC NAME
Panthera pardus
LENGTH 7 to 10 feet
DIET Carnivore
LOCATION
Central Africa and
Southeast Asia

Pardus is Latin for "mottled."

Leopards are extremely strong cats that love hanging out in trees. They'll often lie in wait in a tree's branches, pouncing as soon as prey walks by. To keep their meal safe from scavengers like hyenas, they'll drag whatever they don't eat right away and stash it high up in the tree to finish later. Leopards are also very adept at swimming, sometimes hunting for crabs or fish.

FEROCIOUS AND FAST

Leopards are skilled on land, too—they can run up to 36 miles per hour, a useful skill when stalking prey in tall grasses.

MACAW

SCIENTIFIC NAME
Psittacidae
LENGTH
12 to 40 inches
WINGSPAN
4 feet
DIET Omnivore
LOCATION
South American
Rainforests

Psittákinos means "parrot" in Greek.

Macaws eat all sorts of plants and insects, but their favorite food is nuts. Their specialized tongues are extremely hard and scaly and even have a bone inside them, which makes them ideal for helping to crack hard shells.

These birds are also extremely chatty! They communicate with ear-splitting screams, and some species of macaws that are kept as pets are highly skilled at imitating sounds, like humans speaking.

Wild But True!

Macaw's beaks are so strong they can act like nutcrackers, even crushing whole Brazil nuts.

FORESTS FLYER

Macaws are built for flying through thick rainforests. Their wing flaps are shallow and their bodies and tails are extremely streamlined.

MANDRILL

SCIENTIFIC NAME
Mandrillus sphinx
LENGTH 3 feet
DIET Omnivore
LOCATION Central
Africa Rainforests

Mandrill is a combination of "man" and "drill," a closely related monkey.

Mandrills are the largest monkeys in the world! They're famous for their extremely colorful faces and rears, which males use to attract females—males are more colorful than females and about twice their size. In fact, the more testosterone a male has, the more colorful his face is. Males can even lose their color if they lose "status" within their troop.

Mandrills spend their days foraging for foods like fruits, nuts, seeds and even small animals. Their cheeks have large pockets in them which they use to store extra food for later.

TOOTHY GRIN

Mandrills have extremely long canines, which they often use to defend themselves. However, when one mandrill exposes its teeth to another, it's a friendly gesture.

OKAPI

SCIENTIFIC NAME
Okapia johnstoni
LENGTH 8 feet
DIET Herbivore
LOCATION
Democratic
Republic of Congo

Okapia is from the mammal's native central African name, o'api.

T hough they're much shorter and have striped legs similar to a zebra's, okapi are actually closely related to giraffes. They have similarly shaped heads and the same prehensile tongues, perfect for eating buds and tender leaves.

The okapi's striped legs are also useful, helping it blend into the dappled light that comes through the canopy of the rainforest. Scientists also think the striped legs help young okapi calves pick out and follow their mothers.

IRON STOMACH

Okapi eat more than 100 kinds of plants, many of which are poisonous to humans and other animals.

Wild But True!

The okapi's upright ears are very similar in shape to a giraffe's, helping it pick up on the slightest sounds and avoid predators.

ORANGUTAN

SCIENTIFIC NAME
Pongo
LENGTH
4 to 5 feet
DIET Omnivore
LOCATION Sumatra
and Borneo

In Kongo, mpongo means "large ape."

Orangutans are more independent than other great apes. Young orangutans will stay with their mothers for up to seven years, after which they will go off on their own. However, they can still be very social creatures, and will spend more time together when there is an abundance of fruit in one area—scientists refer to these feeding groups as "parties." Orangutans eat a wide variety of food, including leaves, bark and the occasional meat, but fruit makes up the majority of their diet.

Wild But True!
Orangutans use large tropical leaves to make their own umbrellas and shelters from rain.

AMAZING ARMS

An orangutan's arms stretch longer than their height—usually up to a 7-foot span! It's a useful trait when you spend a lot of time in the trees.

PANTHER CHAMELEON

SCIENTIFIC NAME
Furcifer pardalis
LENGTH
17 inches
DIET Carnivore
LOCATION Northern
Madagascar

In Latin, *furci* means "forked."

Wild But True!
A chameleon's forked feet help it grip narrow branches.

Panther chameleons are famous for their bright and beautiful colors! They don't change color to match whatever they're up against, though. Instead, color changes are usually a way to communicate with other chameleons, or to better absorb heat from light rays.

Chameleons of all kinds mostly eat insects. Their long, extensile tongues can be up to twice the length of their body and are coated in a sticky mucous. This makes them perfect for nabbing any nearby bugs!

CRAZY COLORS

In 2015, scientists discovered that panther chameleons don't control their skin pigment, but instead can tense or relax a layer of skin cells containing nanocrystals. Different colors of light will be reflected off the crystals depending on how close together they are.

RED-EYED TREE FROG

> In Greek, *kalos* means "beautiful" and *dryas* means "tree nymph."

SCIENTIFIC NAME
Agalychnis callidryas
LENGTH 1.5 to 2.75 inches
DIET Carnivore
LOCATION
Central America

To blend into the green rainforest leaves, these frogs spend their days sleeping on the undersides of leaves, with their colorful legs tucked under their bodies. If this doesn't work, they may snap open their red eyes and reveal their colorful limbs, hopefully startling their attacker and giving themselves time to escape.

At night, red-eyed tree frogs wake up and go hunting for food—usually some tasty insects, though they have also been known to eat smaller frogs.

Wild But True!

Red-eyed tree frogs have an extra clear eyelid! It allows them some protections while still letting them see.

CAREFUL CLINGER

Suction cup–like footpads and sticky mucus allow this frog to easily travel on the undersides of leaves.

RING-TAILED LEMUR

SCIENTIFIC NAME *Lemur catta*
LENGTH 17.75 inches
DIET Herbivore
LOCATION Southern Madagascar

In Latin, *lemurēs* means "spirits of the dead."

With a striped tail just as long as its body, the ring-tailed lemur is especially easy to recognize. Unlike monkeys, however, a lemur's tail is not prehensile—it can't be used as an extra limb.

Lemurs are also known to make quite an impression in the dead of night—explorers named them "spirits of the dead" for their nightly howls and bright, glowing eyes.

Unlike many other species of lemurs, ring-tailed lemurs spend a lot of time on the ground instead of high up in the trees. Scientists think this happens because vegetation can be sparse in the trees, requiring the lemurs to travel by ground looking for more.

PUNGENT POWER

When fighting over mates, male lemurs will secrete an especially smelly substance all over their tails and wave it around. Whoever has the stinkiest smell is the winner!

SPIDER MONKEY

SCIENTIFIC NAME *Ateles*
LENGTH 14 to 26 inches
DIET Omnivore
LOCATION Central America and Northwestern Coast of South America

In Greek, *ateles* means "incomplete."

These New World monkeys are just like most others except for one thing: they don't have opposable thumbs, making them "incomplete." They still have an excellent grip and spend much of their time swinging and playing in trees, though. They also find most of their food in trees, including fruit, insects and bird eggs.

Spider monkeys are very social creatures that usually live in groups of around 25 to 35. These primates can also be very chatty, communicating with a wide array of screeches, calls, barks and more.

Wild But True!

Spider monkeys get their name because of how they look while hanging upside down with their limbs dangling.

MOMMA'S MONKEY

Spider monkeys depend on their mothers completely until they are 6 to 10 months old, spending all of their time on their mom's back or stomach.

TAPIR

SCIENTIFIC NAME
Tapirus
LENGTH
29 to 42 inches
DIET Herbivore
LOCATION Central
and South America,
Southeast Asia

Tapir comes from the Brazilian Tupi name, tapi'ira.

These unusual-looking animals look like pigs, but they're more closely related to horses and rhinos. They also have prehensile trunks, like elephants, though the tapir's is much shorter. Tapirs use these trunks to pull the leaves from branches or collect fruit.

Baby tapirs also look a bit like zebras! They often have spots or stripes, helping them to better blend into their environments. These markings will fade by the time the tapir reaches adulthood.

Wild But True!
A group of tapirs is called a candle.

WATER LOVER

Tapirs are excellent swimmers! They often take a dip underwater to cool down and can even dive down to munch on aquatic plants.

THREE-TOED SLOTH

SCIENTIFIC NAME
Bradypus
LENGTH 23 inches
DIET Herbivore
LOCATION Central
and South American
Rainforests

In Greek, *brady* means "slow" and *pous* means "foot."

Three-toed sloths spend just about all their time in treetops. Don't expect to see one swinging around, though—these creatures spend up to 20 hours per day sleeping and stay still for most of their waking hours. In fact, male sloths may stay in the same tree for their entire life!

When they are moving, sloths are usually looking for food or eating. They feed entirely on vegetation, and get all the water they need from fruits.

Wild But True!

Sloths move incredibly slowly, covering just 6 to 8 feet per minute.

SURPRISING SWIMMER

If a sloth is threatened by a predator, its best bet is to drop into the water, where its long arms are put to good use.

TOCO TOUCAN

SCIENTIFIC NAME
Ramphastos toco
LENGTH
2.5 feet (with bill)
DIET Omnivore
LOCATION
South America

In Latin, *ramphastos* means "curved beak."

COLORFUL CAMOUFLAGE

Though its beak looks flashy, the bright colors of the toucan help it blend in with the colorful flowers of the rainforest.

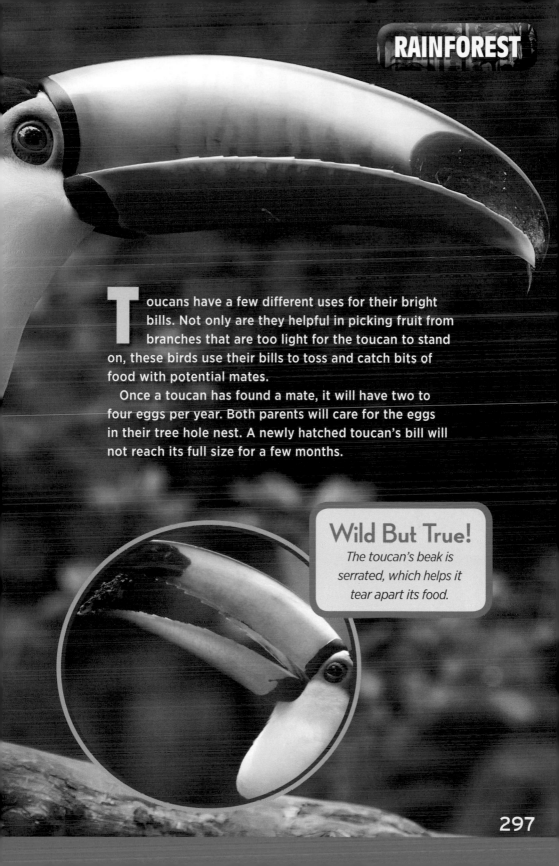

T oucans have a few different uses for their bright bills. Not only are they helpful in picking fruit from branches that are too light for the toucan to stand on, these birds use their bills to toss and catch bits of food with potential mates.

Once a toucan has found a mate, it will have two to four eggs per year. Both parents will care for the eggs in their tree hole nest. A newly hatched toucan's bill will not reach its full size for a few months.

Wild But True!

The toucan's beak is serrated, which helps it tear apart its food.

WESTERN LOWLAND GORILLA

SCIENTIFIC NAME
Gorilla gorilla gorilla
LENGTH 4 to 6 feet
DIET Omnivore
LOCATION Western
Central Africa

In Ancient Greek, *gorillai* means "a tribe of hairy women."

Western lowland gorillas live in groups, or troops, of up to 30 or more animals. Each troop is led by an older male gorilla known as a silverback, so-called for the color of his fur. The silverback decides what time the whole troops wakes, eats and goes to sleep, how far their range is, and even settles any disputes that may arise.

These gorillas are generally very peaceful unless they are provoked or fighting over a female. A gorilla that wants to look intimidating doesn't have much trouble, though. He can stand on his hind legs, beat his chest and roar. If that doesn't do the trick, he will charge at his attacker.

NEEDS A NEST

Gorillas are the only apes that build nests! They build them for both night (to sleep) and day (to nap). Male gorillas often build their nests on the ground, while females may build theirs on the ground or in trees.

Wild But True!

Infant gorillas have small white tufts of fur on their rear to help their mothers and other gorillas in their troop to easily spot them.

QUICK QUIZ

ARE YOU A RAINFOREST EXPERT?

1 Which animals are famous for using tools?
- A. Chimpanzees
- B. Piranhas
- C. Capybaras

2 What percent of a giant panda's diet is bamboo?
- A. 50 percent
- B. 75 percent
- C. 99 percent

3 What is the green basilisk lizard famous for doing?
- A. Eating animals five times its size
- B. Running on water
- C. Gliding between trees

4 Why do chameleons change colors?
- A. For camouflage
- B. To communicate with one another
- C. To look trendy

5 What do scientists call the leader of a troop of gorillas?
- A. Silverback
- B. Greyback
- C. Copperback

6 What is the main reason a blue poison dart frog is so brightly colored?
- A. To attract mates
- B. To blend in with flowers
- C. To warn predators not to eat it

RAINFOREST RIOT

When is it bad luck
to see a leopard?
Whenever it's hungry!

Why do gorillas
have big nostrils?
*Because they have
big fingers!*

Where should a
monkey go when he
loses his tail?
To a re-tailer!

What is a frog's
favorite music?
Hip-HOP!

What do you get if
you cross a centipede
and a macaw?
A walkie-talkie!

Why couldn't the
boa talk?
It had a frog in its throat!

PERUSE THE POLES

About 12 percent of Earth's surface is permanently covered in ice and snow.

AROUND THE

THE ARCTIC SPANS A LOT MORE THAN THE LITERAL NORTH POLE—IT STRETCHES ACROSS THE NORTHERNMOST PARTS OF ASIA, EUROPE AND NORTH AMERICA. ON THE OPPOSITE SIDE OF THE EARTH, ANTARCTICA IS THE FIFTH-LARGEST CONTINENT. NO HUMANS LIVE IN ANTARCTICA, THOUGH SOME SCIENTISTS SPEND TIME THERE IN SPECIAL STATIONS.

An Arctic research station in Norway.

Extreme Cold

Antarctica is the coldest and windiest continent, and because of its low rainfall, it's also technically the world's largest desert! The highest temperature ever recorded there was 63.5 degrees F in 2015, but the average summer temperature is -18 degrees F. Because of this, very few animals and plants live in Antarctica.

WILD WORLD RECORDS

THESE ANIMALS ARE IMPRESSIVE FOR MORE REASONS THAN JUST BRAVING THE COLDEST CLIMATES!

MOST HEROIC
SIBERIAN HUSKY

A group of huskies once saved an entire town in Alaska by pulling sleds carrying some much-needed medicine.

GREATEST DAD
EMPEROR PENGUIN

They don't eat for two months so they can keep their eggs warm.

SMARTEST SHEDDER
MUSK OX

They lose a layer when the warm weather comes.

TOUGHEST TEAM
ARCTIC WOLVES

Not only do they live in the icy Arctic, these wolves hunt together and take care of weaker pack members.

MOST USEFUL TEETH
WALRUS

They use their tusks for self-defense, dragging themselves out of water and even for cutting through ice.

FIVE FACTS ABOUT THE ARCTIC

MOST OF THE ARCTIC ISN'T LAND—IT'S FROZEN WATER! THE PARTS OF THE ARCTIC THAT ARE LAND ARE CALLED TUNDRA.

1 The Arctic can be as cold as –58 degrees F in the winter, but some parts can be warmer than 50 degrees F in the summer.

2 For at least one day per year, the Arctic is in complete darkness. This happens because of the way Earth is tilted.

3 People native to the Arctic are called Inuits.

4 Ice caps contain nearly 70 percent of the world's freshwater. This plays a big role in stabilizing Earth's climate.

5 The Arctic is home to an incredible natural light show known as the Northern Lights or Aurora Borealis.

ARCTIC FOX

SCIENTIFIC NAME
Vulpes lagopus
LENGTH 18 to 27 inches
DIET Omnivore
LOCATION Arctic Tundra

In Greek, *lagos* means "hare" and *pous* means "foot."

Arctic foxes are well suited to their incredibly cold habitats. Shorter ears and muzzles mean they lose less body heat, and furry feet both keep their paws warm and give them better traction on the snow and ice.

Though these foxes are very skilled hunters, prey can be very difficult to find when the weather becomes extremely cold. In these cases, the fox will resort to following polar bears, eating any scraps they leave behind.

CLEVER CAMOUFLAGE

In warmer weather, the Arctic fox's coat will turn a grayish-brown, allowing it to blend into its summer environment of rocks and plants.

Wild But True!

If the Arctic fox cannot reach its burrow, it may tunnel into the snow to make a temporary shelter.

ARCTIC HARE

SCIENTIFIC NAME
Lepus arcticus
LENGTH
19 to 26 inches
DIET Omnivore
LOCATION North American Tundra

In Latin, *lepus* means "hare."

Like other hares, the Arctic hare mostly eats plants, but those can be hard to find under the snow. Luckily for this mammal, its excellent sense of smell helps it locate the woody plants and mosses it prefers to eat—then it just needs to dig down to get to them.

If another animal is after the Arctic hare, it needs to be quick. These speedy animals can bound away at up to 40 miles per hour, and their padded paws keep them from sinking in the snow.

FLUFFY FLOCKERS

During the winter, these hares may gather in extremely large groups—sometimes thousands will "flock" together. When gathered this way, it is more difficult for predators to sneak up on them. The flock becomes synchronized, and will run and change direction all together.

313

ARCTIC REINDEER

SCIENTIFIC NAME
Rangifer tarandus
LENGTH
5.25 to 7 feet
DIET Herbivore
LOCATION
Arctic Tundra

Rangifer and tarandos both mean "reindeer" in Latin and Greek, respectively.

In the Arctic, a reindeer's antlers have a very important purpose: they use them to dig up snow, exposing plants they can eat. Males lose their antlers after the breeding season ends in November, and begin growing new ones in February. Females keep their antlers all winter and lose them after giving birth in May, then begin to grow them again.

Reindeer also have very deeply cloven hooves, allowing their feet to spread out and evenly distribute their weight on the snow.

AMAZING ANTLERS

A reindeer's antlers grow up to 2 centimeters each day! Each reindeer's antler pattern is unique, like a fingerprint.

Wild But True!

Some species of reindeer have knees that make clicking noises as they walk, helping groups stay together in a blizzard.

ARCTIC WOLF

SCIENTIFIC NAME *Canis lupus arctos*
LENGTH 3 to 6 feet
DIET Carnivore
LOCATION North American Arctic Tundra

In Greek, *árktos* means "bear."

When on its own, the Arctic wolf will hunt and eat smaller mammals, like hares, lemming and other rodents. But when traveling in a pack, they will attempt to hunt much larger prey, like reindeer or musk oxen. Though wolves are known for hunting in packs, it still takes a lot of effort for them to take down such a large animal—they only succeed about 10 percent of the time. When they do kill large prey, they eat absolutely everything, even the bones.

Wild But True!

The Arctic wolf is a subspecies of the gray wolf, with smaller legs, ears and muzzles.

PACK PROTECTION

Wolf packs are very tight-knit. The whole pack will help raise and feed new pups, and younger pack members will also care for older or injured wolves.

ATLANTIC PUFFIN

SCIENTIFIC NAME
Fratercula arctica
LENGTH
10 to 12 inches
WINGSPAN
20 to 24 inches
DIET Carnivore
LOCATION North
Atlantic Seacoasts

In Latin, fratercula means "little brother."

These birds spend most of their lives on the icy Arctic waters, only coming to shore in the spring and summer so they can lay eggs and take care of them until they hatch and the chicks are able to take care of themselves. Both parents will take turns keeping the eggs warm and hunting for food.

Otherwise, this puffin spends most of its time flying over the sea, swimming or resting atop the water. They hunt by diving underwater, searching for herrings, sand eels and other small fish.

DEEP DIVE

These puffins can get to depths of up to 200 feet, though they usually stay submerged for less than 30 seconds.

Wild But True!

A male puffin's bill becomes bright yellow, orange and blue during the breeding season.

ATLANTIC WALRUS

SCIENTIFIC NAME
Odobenus rosmarus rosmarus
LENGTH
7 to 12 feet
DIET Carnivore
LOCATION
Arctic Ocean

In Greek, *odobenus* means "tooth walker."

Walruses are famous for their large tusks, which both males and females have. They use them for self-defense, pulling themselves out of the water and cutting through ice.

These giant sea mammals search along the bottom of the ocean floor for food, which they can detect with their whiskers. Walruses mostly eat clams and mussels, but they have also been known to eat small fish and even seal carcasses.

UNDERWATER BELLS

Male walruses have special air sacs in their pharynx (the space behind the nose and mouth) that allow them to make bell-like sounds underwater. Scientists think this helps walruses find one another and warn of nearby predators.

EMPEROR PENGUIN

SCIENTIFIC NAME *Aptenodytes forsteri*
LENGTH 45 inches
WINGSPAN 30 inches
DIET Carnivore
LOCATION Antarctic Coast

In Greek, *aptenodytes* means "featherless diver."

Emperor penguins live in Antarctica, where the temperature can drop to –76 degrees F. To stay warm, they'll huddle in large groups, taking turns being in the middle.

These flightless birds hunt by diving deep beneath the sea—they can swim to an incredible depth of about 1,800 feet. There, they hunt for squid, fish and krill. On land they are much less graceful, and either waddle around or find small slopes to slide down on their bellies.

Wild But True!

Emperor penguins can stay underwater for 20 minutes at a time.

DARING DAD

After a female lays an egg, she immediately leaves to hunt for food. The father keeps the egg warm by balancing it on his feet and covering it with his "brood pouch." Two months later, the egg is ready to hatch and the mother returns with food from her hunt.

HARBOR SEAL

SCIENTIFIC NAME *Phoca vitulina*
LENGTH 4 to 6 feet
DIET Carnivore
LOCATION North Atlantic and North Pacific

In Latin, *vitulina* means "calf-like."

These marine mammals spend about half their time in water, and can spend up to half an hour submerged. They usually only dive beneath the waves for about 3 minutes, however, since they tend to hunt in shallow waters and use their whiskers, which can detect sound waves, to quickly locate prey. Harbor seals mostly eat fish, though they will also eat squid, clams and other shellfish if they come across it.

Wild But True!

Harbor seals are very playful, though they mostly play by themselves or with objects they find, like kelp.

SOLITARY SEALS

Harbor seals are extremely solitary creatures, and most of their forms of communication are used to tell other seals to leave them alone. This includes biting, growling, head-butting and flipper-waving.

MUSK OX

SCIENTIFIC NAME
Ovibos moschatus
LENGTH 4 to 5 feet
DIET Herbivore
LOCATION Arctic Tundra

In Latin, *ovis* means "sheep" and *bōs* means "ox."

Musk oxen eat plants and use their hooves to dig through the snow to get to the grasses, lichens and moss underneath. Unfortunately, this only works in areas with shallow snow, so they often feed near bodies of water.

A musk ox's long, shaggy outer coat and short undercoat give it protection from the cold winds and harsh temperatures of the Arctic. Once summer arrives, the extra undercoat will fall out.

Wild But True!

Newborn musk oxen become independent extremely quickly and are able to keep up with the herd within a few hours of being born.

STRONG DEFENSE

When threatened by wolves or other animals, musk oxen will circle up to protect their young, presenting their sharp horns to any predators.

POLAR BEAR

SCIENTIFIC NAME
Ursus maritimus
LENGTH
7.25 to 8 feet
DIET Carnivore
LOCATION Arctic

This means "sea bear."

Polar bears exclusively live in the icy Arctic. When the weather is cold and ice forms over the ocean, the bears will head out onto the ice and hunt for seals, their favorite meal. Usually polar bears will wait near a breathing hole in the ice for a seal to come up for air, but they also look for dinner by swimming underneath the ice from time to time.

The polar bear's white fur helps it blend into its snowy environment, but its skin is black—the best color for soaking in warm sun rays.

GOOD GRIP

Fur grows on the bottom of a polar bear's paws, which gives them more traction when walking on ice.

SIBERIAN HUSKY

Husky is short for Huskemaw, a variation of Eskimo.

SCIENTIFIC NAME
Canis lupus familiaris
HEIGHT 20 to 24 inches
DIET Omnivore
LOCATION Siberia

Though they're not really wild animals, huskies were bred about 3,000 years ago by the Chukchi, an indigenous people of Siberia, to withstand the frigid weather of Russia and help work in the snow. Today, they're mostly known for their role as sled dogs.

Siberian huskies have a "double coat" of fur consisting of a thick outer coat and a dense undercoat. This allows them to withstand incredibly cold temperatures—they can survive in temperatures colder than −50 degrees F!

SLED SAVIOR

In 1925, 150 sled dogs and their drivers relayed medicine across 674 miles in snow-covered Alaska to save the town of Nome. The record-breaking trip was completed in just about six days.

Wild But True!

A Husky will sleep with its tail wrapped around its face; allowing its breath to keep its nose and face warm.

SNOWY OWL

SCIENTIFIC NAME
Bubo scandiaca
LENGTH
20 to 28 inches
WINGSPAN
4.2 to 4.8 feet
DIET Carnivore
LOCATION Arctic

In Latin, *scandiaca* means "Scandinavia."

OLD AND WHITE-FEATHERED

Male snowy owls become even more white as they age. Females are darker with dusky spots and never become completely white.

Wild But True!

Snowy owl parents are extremely protective of their young, even defending them against wolves.

With their white feathers and ability to withstand temperatures as low as −40 degrees F, snowy owls are built for the Arctic—they were first observed in Scandinavia, and some people even call them Arctic owls.

A snowy owl's favorite meal is lemmings. They might eat up to five of the small rodents each day! They also use their excellent eyesight and hearing to hunt rabbits, fish, birds and other rodents. Once they catch something, they swallow it whole.

QUICK QUIZ
ARE YOU A POLES EXPERT?

1 Why do lots of Arctic animals have furry feet?
- A. To keep them warm
- B. To give them better traction on ice
- C. A and B

2 Which part of a reindeer is unique?
- A. Its hooves
- B. Its antlers
- C. Its ears

3 What do emperor penguins eat?
- A. Moss
- B. Squid, fish and krill
- C. Seals

4 What color is a polar bear's skin?
- A. White
- B. Tan
- C. Black

5 What color are snowy owls?
- A. Mostly white
- B. Mostly brown
- C. Mostly grey

6 What are huskies famous for?
- A. Pulling sleds
- B. Herding cattle
- C. Guarding homes

JOKE CORNER

PUNS FROM THE POLES

Who is a penguin's favorite relative?
Aunt Arctica!

What do you call a blind reindeer?
No eye-deer!

Where are sled dogs trained?
In the mush-room!

What do polar bears eat for lunch?
Ice-burgers!

What do you call a seal in the desert?
Lost!

Where do walruses go to see movies?
The dive-in!

Media Lab Books
For inquiries, call 646-838-6637

Copyright 2019 Topix Media Lab

Published by Topix Media Lab
14 Wall Street, Suite 4B
New York, NY 10005

Printed in Singapore

ISBN-13: 978-1-948174-21-3
ISBN-10: 1-948174-21-9

All images and art Shutterstock except; ALAMY: p18 Nature Picture Library/Alamy; p20 Robert Shantz/Alamy; p22 imageBROKER/Alamy; p25 John Cancalosi/Alamy; p39 imageBROKER/Alamy; p40 Danita Delimont/Alamy; p48 Christopher Stores/Alamy; p49 imageBROKER/Alamy; p63 AfriPics/Alamy; p77 All Canada Photos/Alamy; p89 blickwinkel/Alamy; p94 imageBROKER/Alamy; p96 All Canada Photos/Alamy; p97 Bill Gorum/Alamy; p103 Ann and Steve Toon/Alamy; p105 Images of Africa Photobank/Alamy; p111 EdK/Stockimo/Alamy; p120 Paulo Oliveira/Alamy; p124 Arco Images GmbH/Alamy; p125 Andrey Nekrasov/Alamy; p126 WaterFrame/Alamy; p127 robertharding/Alamy; p128 WaterFrame/Alamy; p130 Adam Suto/Alamy; p134 Helmut Corneli/Almay; p140 Dave Watts/Alamy; p142 Paulo Oliveira/Alamy; p143 Reinhard Dirscherl/Alamy; p148 Andrey Nekrasov/Alamy; p158 WaterFrame/Alamy; p159 WaterFrame/Alamy; p169 Nature Picture Library/Alamy; p171 Sergio Azenha/Alamy; p173 VPC Travel Photo/Alamy; p194 National Geographic Image Collection/Alamy; p195 John Bennet/Alamy; p222 Malcolm Shuyl/Alamy; p227 franzphoto/Alamy; p231 Michelle Gilders/Alamy; p235 Ann and Steve Toon/Alamy; p238 Mark Graf/Alamy; p255 Nature Picture Library/Alamy; p257 YAY Media AS/Alamy; p262 Steve Bloom Images/Alamy; p265 Ernie Janes/Alamy; p275 Steve Bloom Images/Alamy; p299 age fotostock/Alamy; p305 dpa picture alliance/Alamy; p319 tierfotoagenteur/Alamy; p321 WorldFoto/Alamy; p322 Bluegreen Pictures/Alamy; p332 C-images/Alamy; GETTY IMAGES: p43 John Cancalosi/Getty Images; p83 Millard H Sharp/Getty Images; p88 R. Andrew Odum/Getty Images; p91 Bianca Lavies/Getty Images; p98 Tier Und Naturfotografie J und C Sohns/Getty Images; p99 Martin Harvey/Getty Images; p101 S.J. Krasemann/Getty Images; p106 Aditya Singh/Getty Images; p129 Barcroft Media/Getty Images; p131 Westend61/Getty Images; p144 Michael Nolan/Getty Images; p164 Dave Fleetham/Getty Images; p165 Paul Nicklen/Getty Images; p210 Danita Delimont/Getty Images; p230 J & C Johns/Getty Images; p254 Andrew M. Snyder/Getty Images; p266 Tom Soucek/Getty Images; p270 Sylvain Cordier/Getty Images; p273 Bence Mate/Nature Picture Library/Getty Images; p280 Dave Watts/Getty Images; p290 Paulo B. Chaves/Getty Images; p298 Anup Shah/Getty Images; p312 Martin Rietze/Getty Images; p313 Jerry Kobalenko/Getty Images; p320 Steven Kazlowski/Getty Images; ISTOCK: Cover and Title Page: Lion: GlobalP/iStock, Chimpanzee: GlobalP/iStock, Polar Bear: irvingsaperstein/iStock; Back Cover: Kangaroo: Freder/iStock; p2 Placebo365/iStock; p27 stelo/iStock; p45 EcoPic/iStock; p56 zokru/iStock; p69 BirdImages/iStock; p74 mantaphoto/iStock; p84 JohnCarnemolla/iStock; p86 skynesher/iStock; p90 Saddako/iStock; p116 plasticsteak1/iStock; p141 ShotByRob/iStock; p150 4FR/iStock; p172 Kyslynskyy/iStock; p178 skynesher/iStock; p184 jimkruger/iStock; p192 MikeLane45/iStock; p200 surahoto/iStock; p213 Tempau/iStock; p220 stefbennett/iStock; p228 CookiesForDevo/iStock; p229 Lokibaho/iStock; p236 through-my-lens/iStock; p239 songayeNovell/iStock; p242 MidStorm-inc/iStock; p260 JohannesCompaan/iStock; p278 Freder/iStock; p283 undefined undefined/iStock; p288 aiqingwang/iStock; p302 Dougfir/iStock; p311 Ignatiev/iStock; p317 4FR/iStock; p324 the_guitar_mann/iStock; NATURE PICTURE LIBRARY: p237 Nick Hawkins/Nature Picture Library

Smithsonian